LEARN TO CANTONESE 2

An upper beginner's guide to mastering conversational Cantonese

luk6	sik1	waan4	bou2
綠	色	環	保

Green - Recycling

FREE AUDIO!

Written by	Jade Jia Ying Wu
Edited by	Carmen Yeung, Man Wa Kwong
Copy-edited by	Kimberly Newell
Illustration by	Jessica Jiaxin Liang, Jasmine Jia Wen Xu
Design by	June Pham
Voice Recording by	Jade Jia Ying Wu, Kin Ting Ken Hung
Cover Design by	Jessica Jia Xin Liang, June Pham

ISBN-13: 978-0-9996946-3-3
Second Print, 2021

1

To our earth, for its abundant resources
and for letting us celebrate the diversity
of humankind and our languages.

Table of Contents

Message from the Author

Welcome back to the Learn to Speak Cantonese series. Whether you have studied Book 1 from this series or you are struggling to find more advanced Cantonese learning material, I am thrilled that you are continuing with your Cantonese learning journey.

Two years ago, I published the first book of this series, *Learn to Speak Cantonese 1: A Beginner's Guide to Mastering Conversational Cantonese*. Since then I have received many requests from students and readers to continue writing the series because Cantonese learning material for English speakers is always lacking. Further still, learning material for advanced learners is even more scarce.

Out of my native languages, Cantonese has always been my favorite. Not only does it influence my daily life and bond me to my family, it is a remarkably interesting language in its own right. Cantonese has dominated Chinatowns in North America, South America, and Australia for decades. I became motivated to begin this series after reading news articles about the decline of Cantonese in Chinatowns around the world. I believe that Cantonese deserves far greater recognition in both its spoken and written forms as one of the most influential Chinese dialects.

As you may know, Book 1 follows the story of a young man named Gabriel, who had to use Cantonese while meeting his girlfriend's mom for the first time. I was very happy to later discover that Gabriel's story was very relatable for many readers and fans. However, for Book 2, I decided to create a new plotline with new characters to address an issue that I care deeply about: environmental sustainability. There were many reasons why I planned this storyline, but, most of all, I wanted to use the influence I gained from teaching Cantonese to raise public awareness about sustainability. In this book, you will follow the unique story of a polar bear traveling to Hong Kong to share the importance of caring for our planet.

Coincidentally, as I am finishing the manuscript for this book in 2020, COVID-19, a novel coronavirus, has broken out to an extent where no continent has escaped. The impact brought by COVID-19 has unprecedentedly changed the way we live and heightened our sensitivity to the relationship between humans and nature. This has led to the revival of my calling to find ways to protect the environment and treat it better; this is why I decided to address environmental sustainability in this second book.

After reading this book, you will be able to converse in day-to-day Cantonese. In addition to that, you will also be able to advocate for green living in Cantonese. Unlike humans, animals have no ability to advocate for themselves and protect their species from damage caused by mankind. My goal here is to deliver accessible Cantonese learning content in a fun and unconventional way, while also encouraging the world to become more collectively responsible for the environment.

[sai3 soeng6 mou4 naan4 si6,
zi2 paa3 jau5 sam1 jan4]

世上無難事，只怕有心人。

Nothing in the world is too
difficult for one who sets his mind to it.

As this ancient Chinese proverb points out, any deep-seated change takes time, effort, and determination. So be patient with your language learning and don't give up. Good luck and continue to enjoy your journey of learning Cantonese!

Jade Jia Ying Wu
April 2020

Introduction to Regional Cantonese:
Hong Kong and Guangzhou

Cantonese is the most commonly used dialect in Hong Kong, Macau, Guangdong, and parts of Guangxi, China. It originated in Guangzhou (previously referred to as Canton), the southern region of China that is northwest of Hong Kong. Traditionally, it has also dominated Chinatowns in the western world for decades. Although the setting of this book is in Hong Kong, the book uses Cantonese phrases that are universal and can be understood across all Cantonese-speaking regions.

Why is there a difference between Cantonese spoken in different areas? And what are the differences? Just like how English is spoken differently across the world (i.e. British and American English), Cantonese can also be used differently in different regions. Distinct words and regional accents develop due to the influence of local language and culture.

Stretching only 80 miles from Guangzhou, Hong Kong has historically welcomed many immigrants from the region. As a result, it has adopted much of Guangzhou's culture and tradition, such as dim sum and the Cantonese language itself. However, since Hong Kong was ruled as a British colony until 1997, there is significant English influence in Hong Kong's Cantonese.

For example, the phrase "to turn off the light" can be said as 關燈 (gwaan1 dang1) or 熄燈 (sik1 dang1). Both can be understood regardless of where you are from; however, this book uses 關燈 (gwaan1-dang1) as it is more widely used in all Cantonese speaking regions.

The Origins of Cantonese

Cantonese is considered by many linguists as the earliest Chinese dialect. The history of Cantonese can be traced back to China's Qin Dynasty (221 to 206 BC) and Han Dynasty (202 BC to 8 AD, 25 AD to 220 AD), when it is said to be used as 雅言 (ngaa5-jin4), or literary language. Moreover, the rhyming pattern of poetry from the Tang Dynasty and Song Dynasty 唐詩宋詞 (tong4-si1 sung3-ci4) still prevails when read and enunciated in Cantonese.

Although Cantonese shares much of its grammar and characters with Mandarin Chinese, it has an entirely different Romanization and tonal system. Many characters used in Cantonese are not considered formal written Chinese. Therefore, this book will focus on spoken Cantonese with supplemental writing instructions for formal Chinese.

Crash Course 101 on Cantonese Romanization

Chinese is a tonal language, while English is not. What is the easiest way to understand tones? Chinese has many homophones, which refers to words that sound alike but have different meanings. Here are two examples of how Chinese sounds can lead to puns:

4 is considered an unlucky number in Chinese

But why? That is because "four 四 (sei3)" is nearly homophonous to the word "death 死 (sei2)." You see that both "four" and "death" have the same spelling of "sei," and the numbers "3" and "2" coming after "sei" indicate the tone of the character. From this example, you can see that two characters with the same spelling but different tones can indicate very different meanings. See the audio section of the six tones on the next page to read the phonetics and also to hear the difference between each tone.

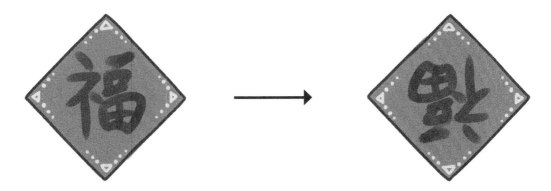

Good fortune "福 [fuk1]"
character hung upside down

This is a common practice of Chinese New Year. But why? It's because "arrival of good fortune 福到 (fuk1-dou3)" sounds exactly the same as "upside down good fortune 福倒 (fuk1-dou3)." From this example you can see, different words can have the same pronunciation, and yet have different meanings.

How can a non-native speaker tell the difference?

I am glad you asked. In 1993, the Linguistic Society of Hong Kong developed an official Cantonese Romanization system called Jyutping, which is similar to phonetics, to help foreign language speakers enunciate every Chinese character in Cantonese—once they learn the initials (consonants), finals (vowels and diphthongs), and tones. There are six Cantonese tones in Jyutping.

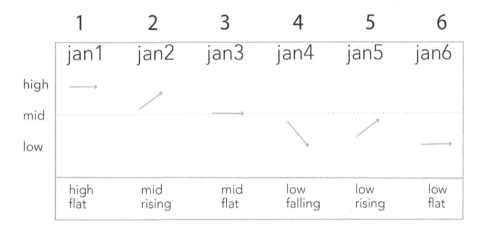

	1	2	3	4	5	6
	jan1	jan2	jan3	jan4	jan5	jan6
	high flat	mid rising	mid flat	low falling	low rising	low flat

What are tones?

Chinese is a tonal language, which means that each character has a fixed pitch pattern. There are 6 tones in Cantonese Jyutping. The digits of 1–6 after the Roman letters indicate the fixed tone of that character.

> As you may notice, tones 1, 3, and 6 are all flat; however, they have different pitches. You can try to associate this with music. When a pianist plays a song, the same musical note can be played on a wide range of octaves on different spots of the keyboard. This is the same theory in tones.
>
> The first, third, and sixth tones are all flat but differ in pitch, with the first being the highest, the third in the middle, and the sixth the lowest.

Jyutping Initials 🔊
(in comparison to English pronunciation)

b boy	p pie	m mike	f five	d dog	t tom	n nice	l light	g go	k kind
ng hang	h hot	gw square	kw quiet	w wind	z joke	c ants	s sing	j yes	

	-	-i	-u	-m	-n	-ng	-p	-t	-k
aa	aa [faa1] 花	aai [taai3] 泰	aau [paau1] 拋	aam [saam1] 衫	aan [baan2] 版	aang [laang5] 冷	aap [laap6] 蠟	aat [baat3] 八	aak [baak3] 百
a		ai [lai4] 黎	au [kau1] 溝	am [kam4] 琴	an [fan1] 分	ang [zang1] 增	ap [sap6] 十	at [sat6] 實	ak [sak1] 塞
e	e [be1] 啤	ei [kei5] 企	eu [deu6] 掉	em [lem2] 舐		eng [peng4] 平	ep [gep6] 夾		ek [sek6] 石
i	i [si1] 思		iu [kiu4] 橋	im [jim4] 嚴	in [pin3] 片	ing [cing1] 青	ip [jip6] 葉	it [git6] 傑	ik [sik6] 食
o	o [to4] 鴕	oi [oi3] 愛	ou [lou5] 老		on [hon3] 看	ong [tong1] 湯		ot [hot3] 渴	ok [sok3] 索
oe	oe [hoe1] 靴					oeng [hoeng1] 香			oek [goek3] 腳
eo		eoi [seoi1] 衰			eon [leon4] 輪			eot [ceot1] 出	
u	u [fu3] 褲	ui [fui1] 灰			un [fun1] 歡	ung [zung1] 中		ut [fut3] 閥	uk [fuk1] 福
yu	yu [jyu2] 魚				yun [jyun5] 軟			yut [syut3] 雪	
				m [m4] 唔		ng [ng5] 伍			

Features of this Book

Before you jump ahead and start reading this book, here are a few important features of the book that you should know:

Study Goal

The main goal of this book is to help you to converse in day-to-day Cantonese. However, there is a significant difference between spoken Cantonese and written Chinese. Although students are not required to know how to read or write all Chinese characters that are used in this book, they will learn the differences between spoken Cantonese and written Chinese for each chapter's key vocabulary. After learning everything in the book, you should be able to form sentences that are useful in everyday conversation and write some of the most commonly used characters.

Audio Track

You can download audio tracks that are supplementary to the book at no additional cost at _www.inspirlang.com/resource_. Audio tracks are provided for Vocabulary, Sample Sentences, and Sample Conversation of each chapter. They are all labeled with a 🔊 sign and organized for your convenience.

Online Flashcards

You can review and study all of the new vocabulary covered in the book by visiting _www.inspirlang.com/resource_.

Vocabulary

In each chapter, there are 3 sections of Vocabulary (A, B and C), all of which are related to the main topic. Audio tracks are available online.

Sample Sentences

Similar to Vocabulary, there are 3 sections of Sample Sentences in each chapter, all of which are constructed using the vocabulary in that chapter. Audio tracks are also available.

Recognizing and Writing Chinese Characters

In each chapter, you will learn to recognize spoken forms of key vocabulary used in the chapter. In addition to that, you will also learn to write the corresponding character in its written form. Sometimes the written form is the same character as the spoken form, and sometimes it is a different character. There are about six to eight characters you will learn to write in each chapter.

Sample Conversations

Sample conversations in each chapter are designed to help the reader learn how to talk to a Cantonese native speaker spontaneously by using the vocabulary and sentence structures learned in the given chapter. This is the last part of the audio track in each chapter.

Cultural Insights

At the end of each chapter, you will learn about some common Cantonese cultural practices, such as sun-drying clothes or using an umbrella in the sun. That is how you can learn not just the language, but also about the culture and its people.

Chapter Exercises

After the section on Cultural Insights, you will have a chance to practice what you have learned in a given chapter with a series of chapter exercises. The questions range from grammatical usage to directly translating the sentences. This is the last section of each chapter.

Characters

Ben

Stormy

Hi, my name is Ben, and I will be your narrator and Cantonese teacher throughout this book. I am a millennial polar bear scientist from Alaska. As a vulnerable species, I am extremely passionate about environmental sustainability. That's why I decided to travel to Hong Kong to advocate for green living.

I chose Hong Kong as my first destination because I have heard that there is a lot of work to be done to improve the environmental conditions there. However, I must learn Cantonese prior to my research and advocacy to better understand the lifestyles of Hong Kongers and fulfill my calling of saving polar bears in the midst of global warming. I will walk you through my Cantonese journey and answer common questions modern bears may have when learning Cantonese.

This is my best friend and neighbor from Alaska, Stormy. Stormy is a courageous and outspoken Pomeranian dog who always encourages me to reach my full potential. He comes from a Cantonese family and is a native speaker. Learning from him allows me to teach you from the perspectives of both a native and non-native speaker. In this book, I am traveling with Stormy to Hong Kong so that you can learn from our experiences and get tips for speaking Cantonese. At the end of each chapter, you will also find Stormy's cultural insights into the differences between Eastern and Western cultures.

Chapter 1

Can I...?

我可唔可以...?

In January, I decided to leave my home in Alaska for Hong Kong to conduct global warming research and advocate for green living. At the same time, I also started learning Cantonese from my best friend Stormy to gain some working knowledge before my travels.

In this chapter, I will address some of the most common questions travelers may have when flying to Hong Kong, such as expressing where to place certain items on the airplane, how to exchange currency when arriving at the airport, and how to take local transportation to get to the final destination. After reading this chapter, you will be able to use spatial terms (left, right, front, and back) to indicate the location of specific objects, use proper terms for money, and ask for directions to confirm your navigation in Cantonese.

Before we begin this new journey, do you remember the most frequently used prepositional verb that we learned from the first book?

喺 [hai2] = at

喺 [hai2] + place = at ...

放 [fong3] = to put; to place

放 [fong3] + 喺 [hai2] + location = to place at ...

Let's take a look at a list of spatial terms that can be used with 喺 (hai2) to indicate where something or someone is.

Vocabulary A 🔊

前面 [cin4-min6] = front

後面 [hau6-min6] = back

上面 [soeng6-min6] = top

下面 [haa6-min6] = bottom

左邊 [zo2-bin1] = left

右邊 [jau6-bin1] = right

行李 [hang4-lei5] = luggage

可以 [ho2-ji5] = can

Let's take a look at how a flight attendant can use these spatial terms along with 喺 (hai2) to tell the passengers where they can place their luggage.

Sample Sentences A 🔊

我喺後面。[ngo5 hai2 hau6-min6]

I am in the back.

我喺你後面。[ngo5 hai2 nei5 hau6-min6]

I am behind you.

你可以放喺呢度。

[nei5 ho2-ji5 fong3 hai2 ni1-dou6]

You can put (it) here.

你嘅行李可以放喺呢度。

[nei5 ge3 hang4-lei5 ho2-ji5 fong3 hai2 ni1-dou6]

Your luggage can be placed here.

你嘅行李可以放喺上面。

[nei5 ge hang4-lei5 ho2-ji5 fong3 hai2 soeng6-min6]

Your luggage can be placed on the top.

你好先生，你嘅行李可以放喺上面。

[nei5-hou2 sin1-saang1, nei5-ge3 hang4-lei5 ho2-ji5 fong3 hai2 soeng6-min6]

Hi sir, you can place your luggage on the top.

Travel Tips: As our airplane landed in the Hong Kong International Airport, we filled out the Arrival Cards distributed inflight. When traveling to Hong Kong, you should request an Arrival Card from your flight attendant if you were not given one during your flight. However, you can always get a new one in the Immigration Hall when you go through customs. The Arrival Card is for the immigration authorities to obtain travelers' information upon entry into the country.

我可唔可以放喺呢度？

[ngo5 ho2-m4-ho2-ji5 fong3 hai2 ni1-dou6?]

Can I place it here?

| 可唔可以 [ho2-m4-ho2-ji5] = Can I...?

Let's take a look at how you can use the numbers that you have already learned to express currency amounts.

Vocabulary B 🔊

港幣 [gong2-bai6] = Hong Kong dollar

美金 [mei5-gam1] = US dollar

唱 [coeng3] = to exchange currencies; to sing

Currency Units		
Dollar	**Ten cents**	**Cent**
蚊 [man1]	毫 [hou4]	仙 [sin1]
1蚊 [jat1 man1] $1	1毫 [jat1 hou4] $0.10	1個仙 [jat1-go3 sin1] $0.01
3蚊 [saam1 man1] $3	3毫 [saam1 hou4] $0.30	3個仙 [saam1-go3 sin1] $0.03
7蚊 [cat1 man1] $7	7毫 [cat1 hou4] $0.70	7個仙 [cat1-go3 sin1] $0.07

	$3	[saam1 man1]
+	$0.30	[saam1 hou4]
+	$0.03	[saam1-go3 sin1]
=	$3.33	[saam1 man1 saam1 hou4 saam1]

	$7	[cat1 man1]
+	$0.80	[baat3 hou4]
+	$0.04	[sei3-go3 sin1]
=	$7.84	[cat1 man1 baat3 hou4 sei3]

As you can see, the last unit "cents" can be omitted to make the phrase less verbose.

Sample Sentences B

呢度可唔可以換唱港幣？

[ni1-dou6 ho2-m4-ho2-ji5 coeng3 gong2-bai6?]

Can I exchange (currency) for HK dollars here?

我想唱港幣。

[ngo5 soeng2 coeng3 gong2-bai6]

I want to exchange (currency) for HK dollars.

我想用美金唱港幣。

[ngo5 soeng2 jung6 mei5-gam1 coeng3 gong2-bai6]

I want to use US dollars to exchange for HK dollars.

今日$1美金可以唱$7.84港幣。

[gam1-jat6 jat1 man1 mei5-gam1 ho2-ji5 coeng3 cat1 man1 baat3 hou4 sei3 gong2-bai6]

Today $1USD can be exchanged for $7.84HKD.

呢個幾錢？[ni1-go3 gei2-cin2?]

How much is this?

呢個$15.70。[ni1-go3 sap6-ng5 man1 cat1 hou4]

This is $15.70.

If you are traveling with a budget, you should always take the airline express, which is available for both buses and trains. However, you will need to purchase an Octopus card or a train ticket beforehand, which you can do at the Tourist Services counter or airport vending machines.

Let's take a look at how you can purchase an Octopus card to take the airline express to your destination, or how you can present your address to the driver if you are hailing a taxi.

Vocabulary C 🔊

八達通(卡) [baat3-daat6-tung1 (kaa1)] = the Octopus (card)

機場快線 [gei1-ceong4 faai3-sin3] = Airline Express

站 [zaam6] = stop; station

下個站 [haa6-go3 zaam6] = next stop

去 [heoi3] = to go to

嚟 [lei4] = to come

地址 [dei6-zi2] = address

Sample Sentences C 🔊

我想要一張八達通卡。

[ngo5 soeng2 jiu3 jat1-zeng1 baat3-daat6-tung1 kaa1]

I would like an Octopus card.

| 張 [zoeng1] is a classifier for cards

我可唔可以用八達通卡呀？

[ngo5 ho2-m4-ho2-ji5 jung6 baat3-daat6-tung1 kaa1 aa3?]

Can I use the Octopus card?

邊度可以搭機場快線呀？

[bin1-dou6 ho2-ji5 daap3 gei1-coeng4 faai3-sin3 aa3?]

Where can I take the airline express?

邊度可以搭機場快線嘅巴士呀？

[bin1-dou6 ho2-ji5 daap3 gei1-coeng4 faai3-sin3 ge3 baa1-si2 aa3?]

Where can I take the airline express bus?

呢部巴士去邊度呀？

[ni1-bou6 baa1-si2 heoi3 bin1-dou6 aa3?]

Where does this bus go?*

| 部 [bou6] is a classifier for automobiles

下個站係咩呀？

[haa6-go3 zaam6 hai6 me1 aa3?]

What is the next stop?

呢部車去唔去佐敦呀？

[ni1-bou6 ce1 heoi3-m4-heoi3 zo2-deon1 aa3?]

Does this bus/train go to Jordan?

As you may have noticed from the last few sentences, a final particle 呀 (aa3) is applied at the end of each question. 呀 (aa3) is the most commonly used final particle that can be used in a neutral statement or question. You will learn more about the reasons and usages of final particles in later chapters.

*Literal meaning: This bus goes where?

唔好意思，你知唔知呢部車下個站係咩呀？

[m4-hou2-ji3-si1, nei5 zi1-m4-zi1 ni1-bou6 ce1 haa6-go3 zaam6 hai6 me1 aa3?]

Excuse me, do you know what is the next stop on this bus/train?

呢個係我嘅地址。

[ni1-go3 hai6 ngo5 ge3 dei6-zi2]

This is my address.

Recognizing and Writing Chinese Characters

Spoken	Written	Definition	Stroke Order	Word Pair
-	士 [si2/si6]	warrior	一 十 士	巴士 [baa1-si2] bus
-	巴 [baa1]	bar	コ 尸 尸 巴	
-	左 [zo2]	left	一 ナ 左 左 左	
-	右 [jau6]	right	一 ナ 才 右 右	
喺 [hai2]	在 [zoi6]	at	一 ナ 大 右 右 在	
嘅 [ge3]	的 [dik1]	's	′ 亻 竹 自 自 的 的 的	
-	前 [cin4]	front	` ′ 一 艹 艼 肻 前 前	

Writing Practice

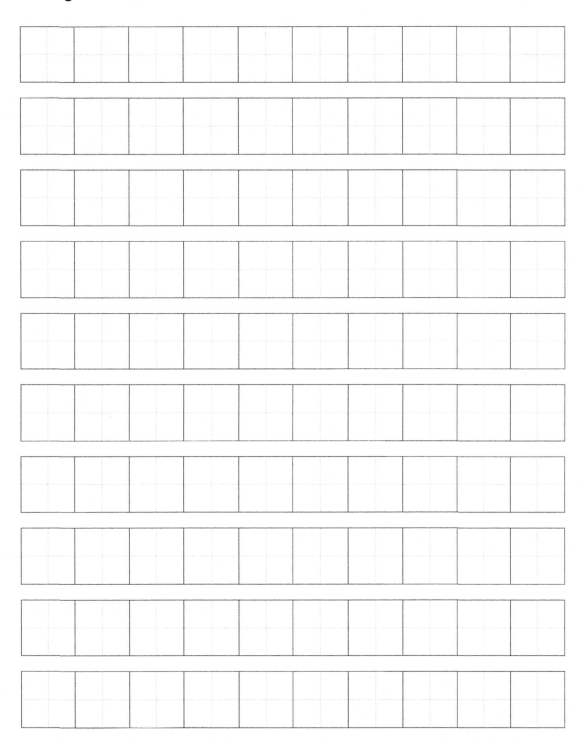

Sample Conversation

-----------------------*On the airplane*-------------------------

Ben *(murmuring):*

你知唔知行李可以放喺邊度呀？

[nei5 zi1-m4-zi1 hang4-lei5 ho2-ji5 fong3 hai2 bin1-dou6 aa3?]

Do you know where the luggage can be placed?

Stormy:

上面。[soeng6-min6]

On top.

Flight Attendant:

你好先生，你嘅行李可以放喺上面。

[nei5-hou2 sin1-saang1, nei5 ge3 hang4-lei5 ho2-ji5 fong3 hai2 soeng6-min6]

Hi sir, you can put your luggage on top.

Ben:

唔該。[m4-goi1]

Thank you.

Flight Attendant:

唔使客氣。[m4-sai2 haak3-hei3]

You're welcome.

Stormy:

我哋要買八達通卡。

[ngo5-dei6 jiu3 maai5 baat3-daat6-tung1 kaa1]

We have to buy an Octopus card.

Ben:

點解呀？[dim2-gaai2 aa3?]

Why?

Stormy:

我哋要搭機場快線。

[ngo5-dei6 jiu3 daap3 gei1-ceong4 faai3-sin3]

We have to take the Airline Express.

Ben *(to the counter):*

你好，我想買兩張八達通卡。

[nei5-hou2, ngo5 soeng2 maai5 loeng2-zoeng1 baat3-daat6-tung1 kaa1]

Hi, I would like to buy two Octopus Cards.

Staff:

每張入幾錢呀？

入 [jap6] = to enter; to add

[mui5-zoeng1 jap6 gei2-cin2 aa3?]

How much would you like to add on each card?

Ben:

每張入200蚊。

[mui5-zeong1 jap6 leong5-baak3 man1]

Recharge $200 on each card.

-----------------------*At the bus stop*-------------------------

Stormy:

Ben, 巴士站喺呢度。

[Ben, baa1-si2 zaam6 hai2 ni1-dou6]

Ben, the bus stop is here.

Ben *(to the driver)*:

唔該，呢部車去唔去佐敦呀？

[m4-goi1, ni1-bou6 ce1 heoi3-m4-heoi3 zo2-deon1 aa3?]

Excuse me, does this bus go to Jordan?

Driver:

去。[heoi3]

Yes, (it goes there).

Ben:

好，唔該。[hou2, m4-goi1]

Okay, thank you.

Cultural insights | Do you need to tip your taxi driver in Hong Kong?

No.

However, most drivers would assume to keep any change less than $1HKD. Voluntary gratitude is a normal practice in Hong Kong, and many foreigners get into this dilemma all of the time. You do not have to be embarrassed for not leaving a tip, but do leave a tip with true gratitude when you really think the service has been exceptional or the driver has been very helpful in giving you travel tips.

Also, it'll be helpful for you to know that an extra $5-$10HKD will be added to your fare if you are storing your luggage in the trunk.

See answers on page #205

Chapter 1 Exercises

1. What is 呀 (aa3) that is applied at the end of a sentence?

   _____

2. What does "我可唔可以 (ngo5 ho2-m4-ho2-ji5)..." mean?

   _____

3. Which preposition can you use to indicate if an object is placed on your left/right/front/back?

   _____

4. What is the unit for every ten cents?

   _____

5. Translate or transliterate the following sentences:

   [ngo5 hai2 nei5 jau6-bin1]

   我喺你右邊。

   _____

   [nei5 ge3 hang4-lei5 hai2 nei5 jau6-bin1]

   你嘅行李喺你右邊。

   _____

   [___ ___ ___ ___ ___ ___ ___]

   你可以放喺呢度。

   You can put it here.

6. Translate the following amounts:

$6.00   _____

$13.90   _____

$87.24   _____

$11.57   _____

My Chinese zodiac sign is...

我屬…

RAT	OX	TIGER	RABBIT	DRAGON	SNAKE	HORSE	GOAT	MONKEY	ROOSTER	DOG	PIG
syu2	ngau4	fu2	tou3	lung4	se4	maa5	joeng4	hau4	gai1	gau2	zyu1
鼠	牛	虎	兔	龍	蛇	馬	羊	猴	雞	狗	豬
2020	2021	2022	2023	2024	2025	2026	2027	2028	2029	2030	2031
2008	2009	2010	2011	2012	2013	2014	2015	2016	2017	2018	2019
1996	1997	1998	1999	2000	2001	2002	2003	2004	2005	2006	2007
1984	1985	1986	1987	1988	1989	1990	1991	1992	1993	1994	1995
1972	1973	1974	1975	1976	1977	1978	1979	1980	1981	1982	1983
1960	1961	1962	1963	1964	1965	1966	1967	1968	1969	1970	1971
1948	1949	1950	1951	1952	1953	1954	1955	1956	1957	1958	1959
1936	1937	1938	1939	1940	1941	1942	1943	1944	1945	1946	1947
1924	1925	1926	1927	1928	1929	1930	1931	1932	1933	1934	1935
1912	1913	1914	1915	1916	1917	1918	1919	1920	1921	1922	1923
1900	1901	1902	1903	1904	1905	1906	1907	1908	1909	1910	1911

As February approaches, every Hong Konger is immersed in festivities to welcome the arrival of the Chinese New Year (Spring Festival). Following the lunar calendar, Chinese New Year usually falls at the end of January or the beginning of February. In this chapter, I will be visiting my neighbor for the new year and chatting about Chinese zodiac signs and pets.

After reading this chapter, you will be able to greet people with well wishes that are used during the Chinese New Year, and tell people your Chinese zodiac sign after learning the names of the animals.

大吉 [daai6-gat1] = propitious

Zodiac sign animal + 年 [nin4] + 大吉 [daai6-gat1] = Good luck in the year of...

豬 [zyu1] = pig

豬年大吉 [zyu1 nin4 daai6-gat1] = Good luck in the year of the pig

Now, let's take a look at how to say all twelve zodiac signs in Cantonese.

Vocabulary A

鼠 [syu2] = rat

牛 [ngau4] = ox

虎 [fu2] = tiger

兔 [tou3] = rabbit

龍 [lung4] = dragon

蛇 [se4] = snake

馬 [maa5] = horse

羊 [joeng4] = goat

猴 [hau4] = monkey

雞 [gai1] = rooster

狗 [gau2] = dog

豬 [zyu1] = pig

Sample Sentences A

我屬豬。[ngo5 suk6 zyu1]

My Chinese zodiac sign is a pig.

我屬羊。[ngo5 suk6 joeng4]

My Chinese zodiac sign is a goat.

你屬咩？[nei5 suk6 me1?]

What is your Chinese zodiac sign?

龍年大吉！[lung4 nin4 daai6-gat1!]

Good luck in the year of the dragon!

蛇年大吉！[se4 nin4 daai6-gat1!]

Good luck in the year of the snake!

In many scenarios, knowing someone's zodiac sign gives you an idea of the person's birth year. To ask someone what his or her birth year is, you can also say, 你咩年出世 (nei5 me1 nin4 ceot1-sai3)?

A common mistake that most non-native speakers would make when they mention zodiac sign is saying "我係...(ngo5 hai6) I am ...." You will never use the "我係... (ngo5 hai6) I am ..." structure to indicate your zodiac sign because comparing a person to an animal can be degrading. For example, saying "我係豬 (ngo5 hai6 zyu1) I am a pig" would imply that you exhibit the undesirable traits of a pig such as being indolent and unintelligent.

Now, let's take a look at some of the other new year wishes you can say during the Chinese New Year.

Vocabulary B

When you express good wishes in Chinese, you typically don't use a personal pronoun such as "I" or "you" because the "I" is already implied when there are only two people speaking. However, you can add the person's title to show respect when you give someone your good wishes. For example, (je4-je2, san1-nin4 faai3-lok6) Happy New Year, Grandpa!

新年快樂 [san1-nin4 faai3-lok6] = Happy New Year!

│ 新年 [san1-nin4] = new year

快樂 [faai3-lok6] = happy

恭喜發財 [gung1-hei2 faat3-coi4] = Wishing you a happy and prosperous new year

│ 恭喜 [gung1-hei2] = to congratulate

│ 發財 [faat3-coi4] = to be prosperous

身體健康 [san1-tai2 gin6-hong1] = (I) wish (you) good health

│ 身體 [san1-tai2] = body

│ 健康 [gin6-hong1] = healthy

龍馬精神 [lung4 maa5 zing1-san4] = Wishing you a year of vitality*

│ 精神 [zing1-san4] = vital

大吉大利 [daai6-gat1 daai6-lei6] = good luck and prosperity

│ 利 [lei6] = profit

*Literal meaning: as vigorous as a gallant horse

Sample Sentences B 🔊

恭喜發財，身體健康！

[gung1-hei2 faat3-coi4, san1-tai2 gin6-hong1!]

Wishing you a year of prosperity and good health!

祝你身體健康。[zuk1 nei5 san1-tai2 gin6-hong1]

Wishing you good health.

祝你豬年大吉。[zuk1 nei5 zyu1 nin4 daai6-gat1]

Wishing you good luck in the year of pig.

祝你2019年大吉大利。

[zuk1 nei5 ji6-ling4-jat1-gau2 nin4 daai6-gat1 daai6-lei6]

Wishing your 2019 is filled with good luck and prosperity.

You can use "祝你 (zuk1 nei5) wishing you" with all of the phrases indicated on the previous page except for 恭喜發財 (gung1-hei2 faat3-coi4).

Vocabulary C 🔊

紅色 [hung4-sik1] = red

黃色 [wong4-sik1] = yellow

藍色 [laam4-sik1] = blue

綠色 [luk6-sik1] = green

橙色 [caang2-sik1] = orange

黑色 [hak1-sik1] = black

白色 [baak6-sik1] = white

啡色 [fe1-sik1] = brown

灰色 [fui1-sik1] = gray

紫色 [zi2-sik1] = purple

粉紅色 [fan2-hung4-sik1] = pink

黑色嘅狗仔 [hak1-sik1 ge3 gau2-zai2] = black puppy

When placing an adjective before a noun to make the noun descriptive, attach 嘅 (ge3) before the noun. 嘅 (ge3) can be used to modify the structure of a sentence.

粉紅色嘅豬仔 [fan2-hung4-sik1 ge3 zyu1-zai2] = pink piggy

啡色嘅馬 [fe1-sik1 ge3 maa5] = brown horse

Sample Sentences C 🔊

我鍾意紫色。[ngo5 zung1-ji3 zi2-sik1]

I like purple.

我有一隻狗仔。[ngo5 jau5 jat1-zek3 gau2-zai2]

I have a puppy.

隻 [zek3] is the classifier for most animals.

我鍾意啡色嘅狗仔。

[ngo5 zung1-ji3 fe1-sik1 ge3 gau2-zai2]

I like brown puppies.

我有一隻白色嘅兔仔。

[ngo5 jau5 jat1-zek3 baak6-sik1 ge3 tou3-zai2]

I have a white bunny.

我女朋友想要一隻黑色嘅狗仔。

[ngo5 neoi5 pang4-jau5 soeng2-jiu3 jat1-zek3 hak1-sik1 ge3 gau2-zai2]

My girlfriend wants a black puppy.

我係一隻白色嘅北極熊。[ngo5 hai6 jat1-zek3 baak6-sik1 ge3 bak1-gik6 hung4]

I am a white polar bear.

| 北極 [bak1-gik6] = North Pole

| 熊 [hung4] = bear

Recognizing and Writing Chinese Characters

Because "吉 (gat1) propitious" is homophonous to "桔 (gat1) tangerine," it is common for Chinese families to decorate their homes with a small tangerine tree, like the one shown in the picture below.

Recognizing and Writing Chinese Characters – cont.

Spoken	Written	Definition	Stroke Order	Word Pair
咩 [me1]	什麼 [sam6-mo1]	what	ノ 亻 仁 什	什麼 [sam6-mo1] what
-	白 [baak6]	white	′ 亻 白 白 白	
-	年 [nin4]	year	ノ 一 二 午 年 年	
-	吉 [gat1]	propitious	一 十 土 吉 吉 吉	
-	羊 [joeng4]	goat	丶 丷 丷 兰 兰 羊	
-	色 [sik1]	color	′ ⺈ ⺈ 色 色 色	
-	狗 [gau2]	dog	′ 犭 犭 犭 狗 狗 狗 狗	

Writing Practice

Sample Conversation 🔊

Ben:

恭喜發財，新年快樂！

[gung1-hei2 faat3-coi4, san1-nin4 faai3-lok6!]

Wish you a happy new year and a year of prosperity!

Neighbor:

恭喜發財，豬年大吉！

[gung1-hei2 faat3-coi4, zyu1 nin4 daai6-gat1!]

Wish you a happy and prosperous year of the pig!

呢隻係你嘅狗仔呀？

[ni1-zek3 hai6 nei5 ge3 gau2-zai2 aa4?]

Is this your dog?

Ben:

係呀。[hai6 aa3]

Yes.

Neighbor:

佢屬咩呀？[keoi5 suk6 me1 aa3?]

What is his Chinese zodiac sign?

Ben:

佢屬兔呀。你呢？[keoi5 suk6 tou3 aa3. nei5 ne1?]

His Chinese zodiac sign is a rabbit. What about you?

Neighbor:

我屬豬。[ngo5 suk6 zyu1]

My Chinese zodiac sign is a pig.

Cultural insights | Chinese New Year Taboos

Taboo 1: No sweeping

Interpretation:
You will sweep away the wealth of the year.

Remedy:
Clean before the new year. If you have to sweep or clean, sweep the direction toward the inside of the house rather than toward the outside of the house. This way you can still keep the wealth and fortune inside the house.

Taboo 2: No congee

Interpretation:
In the past, congee was made because people were too poor to cook a whole meal of rice. Therefore, since congee was once considered food for the poor, you don't want to start your new year with a sign of poverty.

Remedy:
Don't eat congee.

Taboo 3: Avoid hospital visits

Interpretation:
According to superstition, going to the hospital on the day of the Chinese New Year means that the illness may haunt you for the following year.

Remedy:
Although there is no remedy, you should always see a doctor if you are not feeling well.

Taboo 4: No hair cutting or washing

Interpretation:
One of the characters in the Chinese word "頭髮 (tau4-faat3) hair," sounds the same as one of the characters in the word "發財 (faat3-coi4) to be prosperous," You don't want to lose fortune by cutting it off or washing it away on the first day of the year.

Remedy:
Get a haircut and wash your hair before the new year so you can have a new look for the year while not losing any good fortune.

Taboo 5: No negative words

Interpretation:
In addition to curse words, you should also avoid words relating to sickness, death, pain, ghosts, and loss.

Remedy:
Use euphemisms if you have to.

See answers on page #205

Chapter 2 Exercises

1. How many Chinese zodiac signs are there?

    _____

2. How do you ask someone what his/her Chinese zodiac sign is?

    _____

3. Which character do you use after a personal pronoun to indicate possession?

    _____

4. Which character do you use after an adjective and before a noun to modify the structure by making the object descriptive (i.e. fe1 sik1 ___ gau2 zai2)?

    _____

5. Translate the following sentences:

    [____ ____ ____ ____!]

    身體健康!

    Wish you good health!

    [____ ____ ____ ____ ____]

    我有一隻狗。

    I have a dog.

    [____ ____ ____ ____!]

    新年快樂!

    Happy New Year!

    [____ ____ ____ ____ ____ ____ ____ ____]

    我有一隻啡色嘅狗。

    I have a brown dog.

Chapter 3

I have a degree in…

我有一個…學位

In March, after settling down in Hong Kong and falling in love with the city and its culture, I decided to pursue a teaching career at University of Hong Kong where I can simultaneously advocate for green living. While having a conversation with my interviewer, I explained my job-related skills and my teaching experience. After reading this chapter, you will be able to tell someone about your expertise and years of work experience.

Remember in Book 1 we used 我讀… (ngo5 duk6…) to introduce someone to our area of study? Don't worry if you don't remember. In this chapter, we can build on what we have learned to give more detailed answers by telling someone our majors and minors.

主修 [zyu2-sau1] = to major in …

副修 [fu3-sau1] = to minor in …

我 [ngo5] + 主修 [zyu2-sau1] + area of studies = I major (in) …

我主修工程。[ngo5 zyu2-sau1 gung1-cing4] = I major in engineering.

Vocabulary A 🔊

| Lit* = literal meaning

心理學 [sam1-lei5-hok6] = psychology (lit*: the study of the mind)

經濟學 [ging1-zai3-hok6] = economics (lit*: the study of the economy)

統計學 [tung2-gai3-hok6] = statistics (lit*: the study of statistics)

語言學 [jyu5-jin4-hok6] = linguistics (lit*: the study of languages)

環境科學 [waan4-ging2 fo1-hok6] = environmental science

| 環境 [waan4-ging2] = environment

| 科學 [fo1-hok6] = science

生物學 [sang1-mat6-hok6] = biology

| 生物 [sang1-mat6] = living organisms

工商管理 [gung1-soeng1 gun2-lei5] = business administration

| 工商 [gung1-soeng1] = business

| 管理 [gun2-lei5] = management

Sample Sentences A 🔊

If you don't know what your major is in Cantonese, download the Pleco Chinese Dictionary on your smartphone device and enable Cantonese to find the vocabulary you need!

我主修生物學。[ngo5 zyu2-sau1 sang1-mat6-hok6]

I major in biology.

我大學主修心理學同統計學。

[ngo5 daai6-hok6 zyu2-sau1 sam1-lei5-hok6 tung4 tung2-gai3-hok6]

I major in psychology and statistics in college.

我主修工商管理，副修環境科學。

[ngo5 zyu2-sau1 gung1-soeng1 gun2-lei5, fu3-sau1 waan4-ging2 fo1-hok6]

I major in business administration and minor in environmental studies.

我大學主修統計學同經濟學，副修生物學。

[ngo5 daai6-hok6 zyu2-sau1 tung2-gai3-hok6 tung4 ging1-zai3-hok6, fu3-sau1 sang1-mat6-hok6]

I major in statistics and economics in college, (and) minor in biology.

Next, let's learn how to specify your degrees to help you to excel in your job interview.

Vocabulary B

學士 [hok6-si6] = Bachelor

碩士 [sek6-si6] = Master

博士 [bok3-si6] = Doctor

學位 [hok6-wai2] = degree

Sample Sentences B

我有學士學位。[ngo5 jau5 hok6-si6 hok6-wai2]
I have a bachelor's degree.

If someone's degree is in accounting, do you add "in accounting" directly after "bachelor's degree" like in the example next page?

我有一個學士學位~~喺會計~~。

[ngo5 jau5 jat1-go3 hok6-si6 hok6-wai2 ~~hai2 wui6-gai3~~]

I have a bachelor's degree ~~in accounting~~.

Unlike English, additional information is not usually placed at the end of the statement in Chinese. Instead, you would say, "I have an accounting bachelor's degree," or "My bachelor's degree is (in) accounting." Take a look at the examples below.

我有會計學位。

[ngo5 jau5 wui6-gai3 hok6-wai2]

I have an accounting degree.

我嘅學位係心理學。

[ngo5 ge3 hok6-wai2 hai6 sam1-lei5-hok6]

My degree is (in) psychology.

我嘅學士學位係讀經濟學。

[ngo5 ge3 hok6-si6 hok6-wai2 hai6 duk6 ging1-zai3-hok6]

I studied economics for my bachelor's degree.

我嘅博士學位係讀語言學。

[ngo5 ge3 bok3-si6 hok6-wai2 hai6 duk6 jyu5-jin4-hok6]

I studied linguistics for my doctoral degree.

我嘅碩士學位係讀生物學同環境科學。

[ngo5 ge3 sek6-si6 hok6-wai2 hai6 duk6 sang1-mat6-hok6 tung4 waan4-ging2 fo1-hok6]

I studied biology and environmental studies for my master's degree.

我有心理學碩士學位。
[ngo5 jau5 sam1-lei5-hok6 sek6-si6 hok6-wai2]

I have a psychology master's degree.

我有經濟學博士學位。

[ngo5 jau5 ging1-zai3-hok6 bok3-si6 hok6-wai2]

I have an economics doctoral degree.

> Do you remember how to say "to know (a skill)" in Cantonese from Book 1?
> [sik1] = to know (a skill or knowledge)

Now that we learned how to articulate your academic degrees in Cantonese, let's connect it with your work experience to make yourself an outstanding job candidate.

經驗 [ging1-jim6] = experience *(related to knowledge and skills)*

有經驗 [jau5 ging1-jim6] = experienced

我 [ngo5] + 有 [jau5] + 3年 [saam1 nin4] + 嘅 [ge3] + 經驗 [ging1-jim6] = I have three years of experience.

As we mentioned in Chapter 2, if you want to add more details to describe any nouns, place the adjective or detail with 嘅 (ge3) before the noun to modify the structure of the sentence.

Vocabulary C 🔊

工作經驗 [gung1-zok3 ging1-jim6] = work experience

實踐經驗 [sat6-cin5 ging1-jim6] = practical experience

教學經驗 [gaau3-hok6 ging1-jim6] = teaching experience

臨床經驗 [lam4-cong4 ging1-jim6] = clinical experience

理財經驗 [lei5-coi4 ging1-jim6] = financial management experience

Sample Sentences C 🔊

我有三年嘅工作經驗。

[ngo5 jau5 saam1 nin4 ge3 gung1-zok3 ging1-jim6]

I have three years of work experience.

我有兩年嘅會計經驗。

[ngo5 jau5 loeng5 nin4 ge3 wui6-gai3 ging1-jim6]

I have two years of accounting experience.

我有一年做統計嘅經驗，我識用R。

[ngo5 jau5 jat1 nin4 zou6 tung2-gai3 ge3 ging1-jim6, ngo5 sik1 jung6 R]

I have one year of experience doing statistics, (and) I know how to use R.

你有冇做IT嘅經驗呀？

[nei5 jau5-mou5 zou6 IT ge3 ging1-jim6 aa3?]

Do you have (any) experience doing IT?

我有四年做marketing嘅經驗。

[ngo5 jau5 sei3 nin4 zou6 marketing ge3 ging1-jim6]

I have four years of marketing experience.

佢冇一年以上嘅實踐經驗。

[keoi5 mou5 jat1 nin4 ji5-soeng6 ge3 sat6-cin5 ging1-jim6]

He/she doesn't have more than one year of practical experience.

| 以上 [ji5-soeng6] = more than; above

Recognizing and Writing Chinese Characters

Spoken	Written	Definition	Stroke Order	Word Pair
	生 [sang1/ saang1]	raw; living	ノ 一 ニ 生 生	生物 [sang1-mat6] living organism
佢 [keoi5]	它 [taa1]	it	丶 丷 宀 宀 它	
	他 [taa1]	he	ノ 亻 个 仲 他	
	她 [taa1]	she	く 乀 女 如 如 她	
	有 [jau5]	to have	一 ナ 才 有 有 有	
	你 [nei5]	you	ノ 亻 亻 亻 伱 你	
	我 [ngo5]	I	ノ 一 十 手 扎 我 我	

Writing Practice

Sample Conversation 🔊

Ben:

你好，我叫Ben。[nei5-hou2, ngo5 giu3 Ben]

Hi, my name is Ben.

Interviewer:

你好Ben，請介紹一下你自己啦。

[nei5-hou2 Ben, cing2 gaai3-siu6 jat1-haa5 nei5 zi6-gei2 laa1]

Hi Ben, please introduce yourself.

| 介紹 [gaai3-siu6] = to introduce

> The final particle 啦 (laa1) is often used at the end of an imperative sentence as a command or suggestion. You will see more examples of 啦 (laa1) in later chapters.

Ben:

冇問題。

[mou5 man6-tai4]

No problem.

我係美國人。

[ngo5 hai6 mei5-gwok3 jan4]

I am American.

我識中文同英文。

[ngo5 sik1 zung1-man2 tung4 jing1-man2]

I know Chinese and English.

我有生物學嘅博士學位。

[ngo5 jau5 sang1-mat6-hok6 ge3 bok3-si6 hok6-wai2]

I have a biology doctoral degree.

我想喺香港大學教環境科學同生物學。

[ngo5 soeng2 hai2 hoeng1-gong2 daai6-hok6 gaau3 waan4-ging2 fo1-hok6 tung4 sang1-mat6-hok6]

I want to teach environmental science and biology at University of Hong Kong.

Interviewer:

點解你覺得你適合喺呢度教呢？

[dim2-gaai2 nei5 gok3-dak1 nei5 sik1-hap6 hai2 ni1-dou6 gaau3 ne1?]

Why do you think you are a good fit to teach here?

| 覺得 [gok3-dak1] = to think | 適合 [sik1-hap6] = suitable; good fit

Ben:

我好鍾意香港。我想香港嘅大學生了解多啲全球暖化
同點樣幫北極熊。

[ngo5 hou2 zung1-ji3 hoeng1-gong2. ngo5 soeng2 hoeng1-
gong2 ge3 daai6-hok6-saang1 liu5-gaai2 do1-di1 cyun4-kau4
nyun5-faa3 tung4 dim2-joeng2 bong1 bak1-gik6 hung4]

I really like Hong Kong. I want Hong Kong's college students to
learn more about global warming and how to help polar bears.

| 了解 [liu5-gaai2] = to discover; to learn

| 全球暖化 [cyun4-kau4 nyun5-faa3] = global warming

Interviewer:

好，你有冇教學經驗呀？

[hou2, nei5 jau5-mou5 gaau3-hok6 ging1-jim6 aa3?]

Good, do you have any teaching experience?

Ben:

我喺美國有三年嘅教學經驗。

[ngo5 hai2 mei5-gwok3 jau5 saam1 nin4 ge3 gaau3-hok6
ging1-jim6]

I have three years of teaching experience in the U.S.

Interviewer:

你識唔識用R呀？

[nei5 sik1-m4-sik1 jung6 R aa3?]

Do you know how to use R?

Ben:

識。[sik1]
Yes.

Cultural Insights | Not everything needs to be translated to Chinese when speaking in Cantonese

English influence in Hong Kong began with British colonization, which ended in 1997. English has had a mixed influence on the Cantonese vocabulary including loan words, such as 巴士 (baa1-si2) for bus and 士多 (si6-do1) for store, or simply borrowing English words directly, such as "IT" and "marketing" used in this chapter. Words such as "IT" and "marketing" are considered much newer in Cantonese. Although you can find direct translations for such words, they are generally not used in a conversational setting. Therefore, it is very common to hear an English term in a sentence spoken in Cantonese.

Chapter 3 Exercises

1. Which verb can you use to tell someone about your college major?

    _____

2. Which verb can you use to tell someone about your college minor?

    _____

3. What character can you add before a noun and after an adjective to provide more details to the noun?

    _____

4. How do you say "I have two degrees" in Cantonese?

    _____

5. Translate the following sentence:

    [ngo5 jau5 jat1-go3 jyu5-jin4 hok6 sek6-si6 hok6-wai2]

    我有一個語言學碩士學位。

    _____

    [___ ___ ___ ___ ___ ___ ___ ___ ___ ___ ___]

    我有一個經濟學碩士學位。

    I have an economics master's degree.

    [___ ___ ___ ___ ___ ___ ___ ___ ___]

    我有十年嘅工作經驗。

    I have ten years of work experience.

Part I Review: Spring

- To indicate the location of something or someone, you use the preposition 喺 (hai2).

- 可以 [ho2-ji5] = can

- To ask a yes/no question, you use the "verb + 唔 (m4) + verb" structure, i.e. "好唔好 (hou2-m4-hou2) is it good or not good?"

- To ask someone for permission to do something, you might say, "我可唔可以… (ngo5 ho2-m4-ho2-ji5) can I …?"

- 前面 [cin4-min6] = front | 後面 [hau6-min6] = back

- 上面 [soeng6-min6] = top | 下面 [haa6-min6] = bottom

- 左邊 [zo1-bin1] = left | 右邊 [jau6-bin1] = right

- To tell someone your Chinese zodiac sign, you can say "我屬 (ngo5 suk6)… my Chinese zodiac sign is …."

- The classifier for most animals is 隻 (zek3).

- 呀 (aa3) is a final particle that is used to express neutrality and can be used in either a statement or a question.

- To tell someone your major, you can say, "我主修 (ngo5 zyu2-sau1) I major in …."

- To tell someone your minor, you can say, "我副修 (ngo5 fu3-sau1) I minor in …."

- To tell someone your degree, you can say, "我有…學位 (ngo5 jau5 … hok6-wai2) I have a … degree."

- To tell someone your work experience, you can say "我有…經驗 (ngo5 jau5… ging1-jim6) I have … experience."

- To put an adjective or details before a noun, you add 嘅 (ge3) in between. For example, "灰色嘅狗 (fui1-sik1 ge3 gau2) gray dog" and "三年嘅工作經驗 (saam1 nin4 ge3 gung1-zok3 ging1-jim6) three years of work experience."

Sample Paragraph

我叫凱文。我屬牛。我喺紐約返工。我有一個學士學位。我大學主修經濟學,副修心理學。我有兩年嘅工作經驗。我有一隻黑色嘅狗仔。

[ngo5 giu3 hoi2-man4. ngo5 suk6 ngau4. ngo5 hai2 nau2-joek3 faan1-gung1. ngo5 jau5 jat1-go3 hok6-si6 hok6-wai2. ngo5 daai6-hok6 zyu2-sau1 ging1-zai3 hok6, fu3-sau1 sam1-lei5 hok6. ngo5 jau5 loeng5 nin4 ge3 gung1-zok3 ging1-jim6. ngo5 jau5 jat1-zek3 hak1-sik1 ge3 gau2-zai2]

My name is Calvin. My Chinese zodiac sign is an ox. I work in New York. I have a bachelor's degree. In college, I majored in economics and minored in psychology. I have two years of work experience. I have a black puppy.

Sample Exercise

Translate or transliterate the following sentences.

[keoi5 hai2 ngo5 cin4-min6]

佢喺我前面。

_____

[____ ____ ____ ____?]

你屬咩呀?

What is your zodiac sign?

_____

[ngo5 jau5 saam1 nin4 ging1-jim6]

我有三年經驗。

_____

Chapter 4

Although ..., ...

雖然..., 但係...

Since April marks my first four months in Hong Kong, I decided to give my mom a call and tell her how everything has been here. I wanted to tell her how Hong Kong people are and how I've adapted to the weather. In this chapter, I will use the sentence structure we learned in previous chapters and incorporate adjectives to describe someone's traits and state.

After reading this chapter, you will be able to express your feelings and describe the characteristics of a person or place by using the "although ..., ..." sentence structure. You will also learn how to greet someone on the phone.

雖然 [seoi1-jin4]..., 但係 [daan6-hai6]... = Although ..., (but) ...

雖然你好好，但係我唔鍾意你。

[seoi1-jin4 nei5 hou2 hou2, daan6-hai6 ngo5 m4 zung1-ji3 nei5]

Although you are very nice, I don't like you.

Let's take a look at how to describe someone's traits.

Vocabulary A 🔊

高 [gou1] = tall

矮 [ai2] = short

肥 [fei4] = fat

瘦 [sau3] = slender

靚 [leng3] = pretty

醜樣 [cau2-joeng2] = ugly

窮 [kung4] = poor

有錢 [jau5-cin2] = wealthy

後生 [hau6-saang1] = young

老 [lou5] = old

As we have learned in Book 1, when using the verb "to be" in a descriptive statement (i.e., "I am very …"), the copular verb 係 (hai6) is dropped.

As a reminder, 係 (hai6) = am/is/are

So instead of saying "我係好靚 (ngo5 hai6 hou2 leng3) I am pretty," you can simply say "我好靚 (ngo5 hou2 leng3) I very pretty." You can see more examples of this in Sample Sentences A.

Sample Sentences A 🔊

你好高呀。[nei5 hou2 gou1 aa3]

You are very tall.

我好矮。[ngo5 hou2 ai2]

I am very short.

你今日好靚呀。[nei5 gam1-jat6 hou2 leng3 aa3]

You are very pretty today.

雖然我好醜樣，但係我好有錢。

[seoi1-jin4 ngo5 hou2 cau2-joeng2, daan6-hai6 ngo5 hou2 jau5-cin2]

Although I am very ugly, I am very wealthy.

雖然你好窮，但係你好後生。

[seoi1-jin4 nei5 hou2 kung4, daan6-hai6 nei5 hou2 hau6-saang1]

Although you are very poor, you are very young.

Grammar Takeaway
最 [zeoi3] + adj. = the most …
太 [taai3] + adj. = too …

你今日最靚。[nei5 gam1-jat6 zeoi3 leng3]

You are the most beautiful (person) today.

你屋企太靚喇。[nei5 uk1-kei2 taai3 leng3 laa3]

Your home is too beautiful.

When using 太 (taai3) to express excessiveness, the final particle 喇 (laa3) is often added to express certainty.

Now we can take a look at more descriptive adjectives to express your state or feelings.

Vocabulary B 🔊

開心 [hoi1-sam1] = happy

唔開心 [m4 hoi1-sam1] = 1 unhappy; 2 upset

劼 [gui6] = tired

忙 [mong4] = busy

悶 [mun6] = bored

嬲 [nau1] = angry

擔心 [daam1-sam1] = worried

矛盾 [maau4-teon5] = ambivalent

Now we can use adjectives in sentences to describe your emotions throughout the day.

Sample Sentences B 🔊

我好開心。[ngo5 hou2 hoi1-sam1]

I am very happy.

我今日唔開心。[ngo5 gam1-jat6 m4 hoi1-sam1]

I am upset today.

我今日好唔開心。[ngo5 gam1-jat6 hou2 m4 hoi1-sam1]

I am very upset today.

你今日好忙呀？[nei5 gam1-jat6 hou2 mong4 aa4?]

Are you very busy today?

你唔開心呀？[nei5 m4 hoi1-sam1 aa4?]

Are you upset?

我今日好劫呀。[ngo5 gam1-jat6 hou2 gui6 aa3]

I am very tired today.

今日返工好悶呀。

[gam1-jat6 faan1-gung1 hou2 mun6 aa3]

It's very boring at work today.

雖然我今日好劫，但係我好開心。

[seoi1-jin4 ngo5 gam1-jat6 hou2 gui6, daan6-hai6 ngo5 hou2 hoi1-sam1]

Although I am very tired today, I am very happy.

As you may have noticed from a few of the sentences above, a final particle 呀 (aa3/aa4) was applied at the end of each sentence. We learned from previous chapters that 呀 (aa3) can be used in both a statement or a question.

呀 can be pronounced as "aa3" in both a statement and a question to express neutrality and soften the tone of the speaker. When it is used in a yes/no question that shows surprise, 呀 is pronounced as "aa4."

Now, let's learn more terms to describe someone's traits.

Vocabulary C 🔊

好人 [hou2-jan4] = amiable; good person

勤力 [kan4-lik6] = hard-working

認真 [jing6-zan1] = earnest

叻 [lek1] = smart

現實 [jin6-sat1] = realistic

有耐性 [jau5 noi6-sing3] = patient

環保 [waan4-bou2] = eco-friendly

Sample Sentences C 🔊

你好好人。[nei5 hou2 hou2-jan4]
You are very nice.

佢好勤力。[keoi5 hou2 kan4-lik6]
He/she is very diligent.

佢太勤力喇。[keoi5 taai3 kan4-lik6 laa3]
He/she is too hard-working.

你真係叻![nei5 zan1-hai6 lek1]
You are really smart!

| 真係 [zan1-hai6] = 1 indeed; 2 really

香港人真係好現實。

[hoeng1-gong2 jan4 zan1-hai6 hou2 jin6-sat6]
Hong Kong people are indeed very realistic.

香港人最環保。

[hoeng1-gong2 jan4 zeoi3 waan4-bou2]
Hong Kong people are the most eco-friendly.

香港人最唔環保。

[hoeng1-gong2 jan4 zeoi3 m4 waan4-bou2]

Hong Kong people are the least eco-friendly.

雖然香港人好現實，但係好勤力.

[seoi1-jin4 hoeng1-gong2 jan4 hou2 jin6-sat6, daan6-hai6 hou2 kan4-lik6]

Although Hong Kong people are very realistic, they are very hard-working.

Recognizing and Writing Chinese Characters

Spoken	Written	Definition	Stroke Order	Word Pair
-	人 [jan4]	person	丿 人	好人 [hou2-jan4] kind
-	力 [lik6]	strength	丿 力	
-	心 [sam1]	heart	丶 心 心 心	
-	太 [taai3]	too (excessive)	一 丁 大 太	
-	老 [lou5]	very; good	一 十 土 耂 老 老	
-	好 [hou2]	old	く 乚 女 女' 奻 好	
-	呀 [aa3/aa4]	a final particle	丶 冂 口 口' 叮 叮 呀	

Writing Practice

Cultural Insights | How to greet someone on the phone

In earlier chapters, we have learned that 你好 (nei5-hou2) is used to address someone politely. However, in Chinese, there is a different way to greet someone on the phone. When you pick up the phone call, you would say 喂 (wai2) as "hello," followed by the content of the conversation you want to address.

Sample Conversation 🔊

Mama:

喂？[wai2?]

Hello?

Ben:

喂，媽，我係Ben呀。

[wai2, maa1, ngo5 hai6 Ben aa3]

Hi Mom, it's Ben.

Mama:

Ben, 你喺香港點樣呀？

[Ben, nei5 hai2 hoeng1-gong2 dim2-joeng2 aa3?]

Ben, how are you (doing) in Hong Kong?

Ben:

我好好呀。[ngo5 hou2 hou2 aa3]

I am very well.

Mama:

你返工開唔開心呀？

[nei5 faan1-gung1 hoi1-m4-hoi1-sam1 aa3?]

Are you happy at work?

Ben:

雖然返工好忙，但係我好開心。

[seoi1-jin4 faan1-gung1 hou2 mong4, daan6-hai6 ngo5 hou2 hoi1-sam1]

Although going to work is very busy, I am very happy.

Mama:

太好喇！你嘅學生點樣呀？

[taai3 hou2 laa3! nei5 ge3 hok6-saang1 dim2-joeng2 aa3?]

That's great! How are your students?

Ben:

香港嘅大學生好勤力同好認真。

[hoeng1-gong2 ge3 daai6-hok6-saang1 hou2 kan4-lik6 tung4 hou2 jing6-zan1]

College students in Hong Kong are very hard-working and earnest.

Cultural Insights | Gender equality in Hong Kong: Breaking the stereotype of Kong Girls and Kong Boys

港女 (gong2-neoi2) literally means "Kong Girl," or a woman who is from Hong Kong. However, it is actually used as a stereotypical label for women who exhibit undesirable traits such as being materialistic and self-centered. When someone is being called a 港女 (gong2-neoi2), it is usually degrading and humiliating. For a woman who remains unmarried in her late 20s, another label is also attached, 剩女 (sing6-neoi2), or spinster in English.

港男 (gong2-naam4) literally means "Kong Boy." This, however, is more neutral, or less humiliating than 港女 (gong2-neoi2). It can refer to a man who is from Hong Kong, though it may also exhibit other undesirable traits such as being socially awkward. For a man who remains unmarried after 35, he can be called 鑽石王老五 (zyun3-sek6 wong4-lou5-ng5), a Golden Bachelor, which literally means a "diamond bachelor."

As the most westernized region in Asia, Hong Kong still faces severe gender discrimination. The Equal Opportunity Commission's 2018 report found that more than 50% of Hong Kong employers said that they would not hire women with children. This is fascinating data that illustrates Hong Kong's workplace outlook for women. To stop gender discrimination, no woman should be associated with labels such as 港女 (gong2-neoi2) and 剩女 (sing6-neoi2). Instead, each individual should be celebrated regardless of their traits or family situation.

See answers on page #206

Chapter 4 Exercises

1. Do you use the copular verb "係 (hai6) is/am/are" when you describe someone's state, such as, "You are very hard-working?"

   _____

2. What is "呀 (aa3/aa4)?"

   _____

3. Do you use 呀 (aa4) at the end of a statement or question?

   _____

4. Can you use 呀 (aa3) after both a statement and a question?

   _____

5. Translate or transliterate the following sentences:

   [ngo5 hou2 nau1]

   我好嬲。

   _____

   [keoi5 gam1-jat6 hou2 mong4]

   佢今日好忙。

   _____

   [___ ___ ___ ___ ___ ___]

   我今日太劫喇。

   I am too tired today.

Chapter 5

There are ... nearby

呢度附近有...

In May, after having really enjoyed my past five months in Hong Kong, both Stormy and I decided that we should talk to a real estate agent to find a home with a long-term lease.

In this chapter, you will learn how to say different parts of an apartment unit, the standard metric system used in Hong Kong, and the three main districts of the city. After reading this chapter, you will be able to ask about the available rooms in an apartment, the size of the unit, and whether it is far or close to different locations. You will also learn about some of the common practices in Hong Kong households that you may consider a culture shock.

Now, let's learn the names of different parts of a house so you can find an ideal place to rent.

Vocabulary A 🔊

屋 [uk1] = 1 house; 2 apartment; 3 studio

房 [fong2] = room

單位 [daan1-wai2] = (apartment) unit

睡房 [seoi6-fong2] = bedroom

廁所 [ci3-so2] = toilet

洗手間 [sai2-sau2-gaan1] = bathroom

浴室 [juk6-sat1] = bathroom (for bathing)

廚房 [cyu4-fong2] = kitchen

飯廳 [faan6-teng1] = dining room

客廳 [haak3-teng1] = living room

露台 [lou6-toi4] = balcony

地下室 [dei6-haa6-sat1] = basement

Sample Sentences A 🔊

呢度有兩個睡房。

[ni1-dou6 jau5 loeng5-go3 seoi6-fong2]

There are two bedrooms here.

呢間屋有一個廚房。

[ni1-gaan1 uk1 jau5 jat1-go3 cyu4-fong2]

This house has one kitchen.

我屋企冇露台。

[ngo5 uk1-kei2 mou5 lou6-toi4]

My house has no balcony.

呢度有冇飯廳呀？

[ni1-dou6 jau5-mou5 faan6-teng1 aa3?]

Is there a dining room here?

呢間屋有3間房。

[ni1-gaan1 uk1 jau5 saam1-gaan1 fong2]

This house has three rooms.

間 (gaan1) is a classifier specifically for shops, offices, buildings, houses, and rooms other than the generic classifier 個 (go3).

我想要露臺。

[ngo5 soeng2 jiu3 lou6-toi4]

I want a balcony.

Vocabulary B 🔊

呎 [cek3] = foot

平方呎 [ping4-fong1 cek3] = square foot (ft^2)

米 [mai5] = meter

平方米 [ping4-fong1 mai5] = square meter (m^2)

吋 [cyun3] = inch

平方吋 [ping4-fong1 cyun3] = square inch (in^2)

Before moving on to the measurements of the room, let's review numbers in Cantonese on the next page and learn higher digit numbers.

幾(多)米 [gei2 (do1) mai5] = how many meters

幾(多)平方米 [gei2 (do1) ping4-fong1 mai5] = how many square meters

幾(多)呎 [gei2 (do1) cek3] = how many feet

幾(多)平方呎 [gei2 (do1) ping4-fong1 cek3] = how many square feet

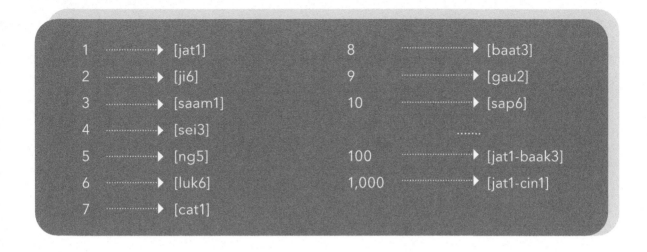

1	⋯⋯▶ [jat1]	8	⋯⋯▶ [baat3]
2	⋯⋯▶ [ji6]	9	⋯⋯▶ [gau2]
3	⋯⋯▶ [saam1]	10	⋯⋯▶ [sap6]
4	⋯⋯▶ [sei3]	⋯⋯	
5	⋯⋯▶ [ng5]	100	⋯⋯▶ [jat1-baak3]
6	⋯⋯▶ [luk6]	1,000	⋯⋯▶ [jat1-cin1]
7	⋯⋯▶ [cat1]		

$$\begin{array}{rl} & \textbf{(}9\ [\text{gau2}]\textbf{)} \\ \textbf{x} & \textbf{(}100\ [\text{baak3}]\textbf{)} \\ \hline = & 900\ [\text{gau2-baak3}] \end{array}$$

$$\begin{array}{rl} & \textbf{(}4\ [\text{sei3}]\ \textbf{x}\ 100\ [\text{baak3}]\textbf{)} \\ + & \textbf{(}7\ [\text{cat1}]\ \textbf{x}\ 10\ [\text{sap6}]\textbf{)} \\ + & \textbf{(}6\ [\text{luk6}]\textbf{)} \\ \hline = & 476\ [\text{sei3-baak3 cat1-sap6-luk6}] \end{array}$$

$$\begin{array}{rl} & \textbf{(}1\ [\text{jat1}]\ \textbf{x}\ 1000\ [\text{cin1}]\textbf{)} \\ + & \textbf{(}8\ [\text{baat3}]\ \textbf{x}\ 100\ [\text{baak3}]\textbf{)} \\ + & \textbf{(}5\ [\text{ng5}]\ \textbf{x}\ 10\ [\text{sap6}]\textbf{)} \\ + & \textbf{(}2\ [\text{ji6}]\textbf{)} \\ \hline = & 1,852\ [\text{jat1-cin1 baat3-baak3 ng5-sap6-ji6}] \end{array}$$

Sample Sentences B 🔊

呢間屋有幾多平方呎呀？

[ni1-gaan1 uk1 jau5 gei2-do1 ping4-fong1 cek3 aa3?]

How many square feet does this house have?

呢間屋有800平方呎。

[ni1-gaan1 uk1 jau5 baat3-baak3 ping4-fong1 cek3]

This house has 800 square feet.

我屋企有923平方呎。

[ngo5 uk1-kei2 jau5 gau2-baak3 ji6-sap6-saam1 ping4-fong3 cek3]

My house has 923 square feet.

呢間房幾大呀？

[ni1-gaan1 fong2 gei2 daai6 aa3?]

How big is this room? / What's the size of this room?

呢間屋有一間房，350(平方)呎。

[ni1-gaan1 uk1 jau5 jat1-gaan1 fong2, saam1-baak3 ng5-sap6 (ping4-fong1) cek3]

This house has one room, 350 (square) feet.

"平方呎 (ping4-fong1 cek3) square feet" is often abbreviated as "呎 (cek3)" on ads and in conversations. It can be understood from context.

呢間屋一個月8000蚊租金。

[ni1-gaan1 uk1 jat1-go3 jyut6 baat3-cin1 man1 zou1-gam1]

The house's monthly rent is $8,000.

| 租金 [zou1-gam1] = rent amount

Besides the interior of the house, the environment is also very important. Let's take a look at the amenities near this apartment.

Vocabulary C 🔊

附近 [fu6-gan6] = nearby

裏面 [leoi5-min6] = inside

出面 [ceot1-min6] = outside

香港島 [hoeng1-gong2 dou2] = Hong Kong Island

新界 [san1-gaai3] = New Territories

九龍 [gau2-lung4] = Kowloon

遠 [jyun5] = far

近 [kan5] = near

Sample Sentences C 🔊

我住喺九龍。[ngo5 zyu6 hai2 gau2-lung4]

I live in Kowloon.

我想去香港島。

[ngo5 soeng2 heoi3 hoeng1-gong2 dou2]

I want to go to Hong Kong Island.

呢度附近有咩呀？[ni1-dou6 fu6-gan6 jau5 me1 aa3?]

What is near here?

呢度附近有冇茶餐廳呀？

[ni1-dou6 fu6-gan6 jau5-mou5 caa4-caan1-teng1 aa3?]

Are there any Hong Kong-style café restaurants nearby?

| 茶餐廳 [caa4-caan1-teng1] = Hong Kong-style café restaurant

呢度去港島好遠。

[ni1-dou6 heoi3 gong2-dou2 hou2 jyun5]

Hong Kong Island is very far to go to from here.

香港島 (hoeng1-gong2 dou2), Hong Kong Island, is often abbreviated as 港島 (gong2-dou2).

呢度返工好近。[ni1-dou6 faan1-gung1 hou2 kan5]

Work is very near to here.

九龍好近呢度。[gau2-lung4 hou2 kan5 ni1-dou6]

Kowloon is very near to here.

Recognizing and Writing Chinese Characters

Spoken	Written	Definition	Stroke Order	Word Pair
-	大 [daai6]	big	一 ナ 大	
-	方 [fong1]	square	丶 一 亠 方	平方 [ping4-fong1] squared(²)
-	平 [peng4/ping4]	flat	一 丶 丆 立 平	平方 [ping4-fong1] squared(²)
-	米 [mai5]	meter; uncooked rice	丶 丿 一 十 半 米	十米 [sap6 mai5] ten meters
-	呎 [cek3]	foot (metric)	丨 冂 口 叮 叩 叺 呎	
-	房 [fong2]	room	丶 一 亠 户 戶 房 房	
係 [hai6]	是 [si6]	yes; am; is; are	丨 冂 日 日 旦 早 昌 是 是	

Writing Practice

Sample Conversation

Ben:

你好，我想租屋。

[nei5 hou2, ngo5 soeng2 zou1 uk1]

Hi, I would like to rent a house/apartment.

Agent:

你好先生，你想租邊度呀？

[nei5-hou2 sin1-saang1, nei5 soeng2 zou1 bin1-dou6 aa3?]

Hi sir, where would you like to rent?

Ben:

我想租喺九龍。

[ngo5 soeng2 zou1 hai2 gau2-lung4]

I would like to rent in Kowloon.

Agent:

你睇下呢個單位。

[nei5 tai2 haa5 ni1-go3 daan1-wai2]

Take a look at this (apartment) unit.

Ben:

呢個單位係喺邊度呀？

[ni1-go3 daan1-wai2 hai6 hai2 bin1-dou6 aa3?]

Where is this unit?

Agent:

喺油麻地。[hai2 jau4-maa4-dei2]

It's in Yau Ma Tei.

呢度去旺角同佐敦好近。

[ni1-dou6 heoi3 wong6-gok3 tung4 zo2-deon1 hou2 kan5]

Mong Kok and Jordan are very near to here.

Remember
係 (hai6) = is/am/are
喺 (hai2) = at

Ben:

呢間屋幾大呀？

[ni1-gaan1 uk1 gei2 daai6 aa3?]

How big is this unit?

Agent:

呢間屋有940呎。

[ni1-gaan1 uk1 jau5 gau2-baak3 sei3-sap6 cek3]

This unit has 940 (square) feet.

有兩個睡房、一個廚房、一個客廳、一個浴室、同一個露台。

[jau5 loeng5-go3 seoi6-fong2, jat1-go3 cyu4-fong2, jat1-go3 haak3-teng1, jat1-go3 juk6-sat1, tung4 jat1-go3 lou6-toi4]

There are two bedrooms, one kitchen, one living room, one bathroom, and one balcony.

Ben:

呢度附近有咩呀？

[ni1-dou6 fu6-gan6 jau5 me1 aa3?]

What is around here?

Agent:

呢度附近有好多茶餐廳。

[ni1-dou6 fu6-gan6 jau5 hou2-do1 caa4-caan1-teng1]

There are many Hong Kong-style café restaurants nearby.

Ben:

一個月幾錢呀？

[jat1-go3 jyut6 gei2-cin2 aa3?]

How much money is it for a month?

Agent:

好平，一個月27,000蚊

[hou2 peng4, jat1-go3 jyut6 ji6-maan6 cat1-cin1 man1]

It's very cheap, $27,000 for a month.

Ben *(murmuring to Stormy):*

你覺得點呀？[nei5 gok3-dak1 dim2 aa3?]

What do you think?

| 覺得 [gok3-dak1] = to think

Stormy:

我覺得唔錯。[ngo5 gok3-dak1 m4-co3]

I think it's not bad.

Cultural Insights | Laundry hanging in Hong Kong

Although using washing machines is standard in Hong Kong, you will seldom find places that sell electric dryers. To dry clothes, residents usually hang their clothes outside of apartment windows or on the balcony if there is one. Hanging laundry to dry is a very common practice in China, because sun-drying is cost-efficient and energy-efficient.

Q: Why don't people use electric dryers?

A: Sun-drying is free, great for maintaining the clothing condition, and excellent for saving the environment.

Q: But what about intimates?

A: Depending on the resources and space that you have, intimates can be hung the same way as other clothes—outside the apartment windows. This may be hard to get used to, as it is often considered uncivilized to show intimates to the public. However, hanging intimates outside the window is not a mainstream practice in Hong Kong, especially for people who are above middle-class. Hanging clothes on the balcony is more common, since the balcony is considered private space. Finding apartment units with dryers is hard in China, and those housing units are usually more expensive because they are designed to be rented out to foreigners.

It is all about adapting to different cultures and environments. Sun-drying laundry is good for the environment, and when it's good for the environment, it's good for polar bears.

See answers on page #207

Chapter 5 Exercises

1. How do you tell people "I live at …?"

   _____

2. What is the classifier for houses, shops, buildings, offices and rooms?

   _____

3. What is the most common metric unit for an area of space in Hong Kong?

   _____

4. Translate or transliterate the following sentences:

   [ni1-go3 hai6 cyu4-fong2]

   呢個係廚房。

   _____

   [go2-gaan1 hai6 juk6-sat1]

   嗰間係浴室。

   _____

   [___ ___ ___ ___ ___]

   我住喺九龍。

   I live in Kowloon.

5. Translate the following numbers to Jyutping:

500	_____	5,700	_____
530	_____	5,780	_____
536	_____	5,789	_____

Where are you going to eat lunch today?

你今日去邊度食晏呀？

麵類 Noodle

炒麵 Chow Mein $55
caau2-min6

撈麵 Lo Mein $57
lou1-min6

餛飩麵 Wonton Noodle Soup $60
wan4-tan1 min6

牛肉麵 Beef Noodle Soup $58
ngau4-juk6 min6

午餐 Rice

煲仔飯 Clay Pot Rice $65
bou1-zai2 faan6

雞髀飯 Chicken Drumstick Rice ... $65
gai1 bei2 faan6

豬扒飯 Pork Chop Rice $70
zyu1-paa2 faan6

叉燒飯 Roast Pork Rice $67
caa1-siu1 faan6

早餐 Breakfast

A餐: 西多士 French Toast $35
A caan1: sai1 do1-si2

B餐: 腿治 Ham Sandwich $40
B caan1: teoi2 zi6

C餐: 麥皮 Oatmeal $20
C caan1: mak6-pei4

雞粥 chicken Congee $42
gai1 zuk1

點心 Dimsum

蝦餃 Shrimp Dumplings $30
haa1-gaau2

燒賣 Steamed Dumpling $32
siu1-maai2

蝦腸 Shrimp Rice Noodle Roll $35
haa1 coeng2

飲品 Drinks

茶 tea $15
caa4

奶茶 Milk Tea $18
naai5-caa4

咖啡 Coffee $18
gaa3-fe1

凍飲+$2

30年傳承 —
Since 1990 —

好好

茶餐廳

InspirLang Cafe

地址：芝麻街7棟201號

營業時間
8:00a.m. ~ 10:00p.m.

好味美食、好品人生

外賣電話
929-322-4578

In June, after six months of living in Hong Kong, I have already fallen in love with Cantonese delicacies and the local cuisine. In this chapter, I will introduce to you different types of Cantonese restaurants and some typical orders.

After reading this chapter, you will be able to order food in a Hong Kong-style café restaurant as well as any restaurant where Cantonese is used.

Vocabulary A 🔊

餐 [caan1] = meal

早餐 [zou2-caan1] = breakfast

午餐 [ng5-caan1] = lunch

晚餐 [maan5-caan1] = dinner

餐廳 [caan1-teng1] = restaurant

茶餐廳 [caa4-caan1-teng1] = Hong Kong-style café restaurant

冰室 [bing1-sat1] = an earlier version of 茶餐廳 (caa4-caan1-teng1) that also provides desserts and frozen treats

酒樓 [zau2-lau4] / 茶樓 [caa4-lau4] = Chinese restaurant

大排檔 [daai6-paai4-dong3] = food stall

Classifiers
A common classifier for buildings and accommodations is 間 (gaan1), as we learned in Chapter 5.

For example:

一間餐廳 [jat1-gaan1 caan1-teng1] = one restaurant

一間冰室 [jat1-gaan1 bing1-sat1] = one traditional Hong Kong-style café restaurant

一間酒樓 [jat1-gaan1 zau2-lau4] = one Chinese restaurant

Sample Sentences A 🔊

我今日午餐食咗好多嘢。

[ngo5 gam1-jat6 ng5-caan1 sik6 zo2 hou2-do1 je5]

I ate a lot for lunch today.

| 嘢 [je5] = thing

你今日午餐食咗咩呀？

[nei5 gam1-jat6 ng5-caan1 sik6 zo2 me1 aa3?]

What did you eat for lunch today?

你今日去邊度食晏呀？

[nei5 gam1-jat6 heoi3 bin1-dou6 sik6 aan3 aa3?]

Where are you going to eat lunch today?

In addition to 午餐 (ng5-caan1), people also use 食晏 (sik6 aan3) colloquially for "eating lunch." For example, 我今日喺ABC餐廳食晏 (ngo5 gam1-jat6 hai2 ABC caan1-teng1 sik6 aan3), I ate at ABC restaurant today.

你今日去咗邊度食晏呀？

[nei5 gam1-jat6 heoi3 zo2 bin1-dou6 sik6 aan3 aa3?]

Where did you go to eat lunch today?

呢間餐廳嘅嘢好好味。

[ni1-gaan1 caan1-teng1 ge3 je5 hou2 hou2-mei6]

This restaurant's food is very delicious.

你唔想去呢間大排檔呀？

[nei5 m4 soeng2 heoi3 ni1-gaan1 daai6-paai4-dong3 aa4?]

You don't want to go to this food stall?

As a reminder, 呀 (aa4) is used at the end of a yes/no question to express surprise and unexpectation.

佢早餐想唔想食茶餐廳呀？

[keoi5 zou2-caan1 soeng2-m4-soeng2 sik6 caa4-caan1-teng1 aa3?]

Does he want to go to a Hong Kong-style café for breakfast?*

點解我哋晚餐去嗰間酒樓呀？

[dim2-gaai2 ngo5-dei6 maan5-caan1 heoi3 go2-gaan1 zau2-lau4 aa3?]

Why are we going to have dinner at that Chinese restaurant?

After choosing the restaurant, let's learn how to customize our food order and comment on the quality and taste of the food.

Vocabulary B 🔊

甜 [tim4] = sweet

酸 [syun1] = sour

苦 [fu2] = bitter

辣 [laat6] = spicy

鹹 [haam4] = salty

走... [zau2] = no ...

走甜 [zau2 tim4] = no sugar

多... [do1] = more ...

多甜 [do1 tim4] = more sugar

少... [siu2] = less ...

少甜 [siu2 tim4] = less sugar

走 (zau2) from the last chapter literally means "to go" or "to leave." An easier way to remember "no sugar" is, "All the sweetness needs to go away!"

You can always use these phrases to customize your food order with more or less of the ingredients which you desire.

*Literal meaning: For his breakfast, does he want or doesn't he want to eat (at a) Hong Kong-style café restaurant?

Sample Sentences B 🔊

呢杯奶茶好甜呀。

[ni1-bui1 naai5-caa4 hou2 tim4 aa3]

This milk tea is very sweet.

我杯鴛鴦好甜呀。

[ngo5 bui1 jyun1-joeng1 hou2 tim4 aa3]

My (cup of) Yuenyeung is very sweet.

| 鴛鴦 [jyun1-joeng1] = Yuenyeung; coffee with milk tea is a common beverage you can find in any Hong Kong-style café restaurant or bakery.

呢杯鴛鴦太甜喇！

[ni1-bui1 jyun1-joeng1 taai3 tim4 laa3!]

This coffee with milk tea is too sweet!

Besides indicating the state of change and certainty of evaluation, 喇 (laa3) can also be used to express an unpleasant exclamation or assertion, which is the case here.

我想要一杯鴛鴦，走甜。

[ngo5 soeng2 jiu3 jat1-bui1 jyun1-joeng1, zau2 tim4]

I would like a coffee with milk tea and no sugar.

我想要一個牛肉飯走蔥。

[ngo5 soeng2 jiu3 jat1-go3 ngau4-juk6 faan6 zau2 cung1]

I would like one order of beef rice with no scallions.

| 蔥 [cung1] = scallion

唔該，我哋想要兩份咖喱飯少辣。

[m4-goi1, ngo5-dei6 soeng2 jiu3 loeng5-fan6 gaa3-lei1 faan6 siu2 laat6]

Excuse me, we would like two servings of curry rice that is less spicy.

| 咖喱 [gaa3-lei1] = curry

點解你碗雞肉面有咁多蔥呀？

[dim2-gaai2 nei5 wun2 gai1-juk6 min6 jau5 gam3-do1 cung1 aa3?]

Why does your bowl of chicken noodles have so many scallions?

因為我好鍾意食蔥呀。

[jan1-wai6 ngo5 hou2 zung1-ji3 sik6 cung1 aa3]

Because I really like to eat scallion.

In Chapter 5, we learned that different area units are used in Hong Kong compared to the U.S. The variation of units is not only applied to area, but also mass. Take a look at the following examples in Vocabulary C.

Vocabulary C 🔊

磅 [bong6] = pound

一磅 [jat1 bong6] = one pound

斤 [gan1] = catty (a unit of mass)

一斤 [jat1 gan1] = one catty

半斤 [bun3 gan1] = half catty

Because "磅 (bong6) pound" is already a unit, there is no need to place another classifier before it.

"斤 (gan1) catty" is a more common and traditional mass unit used in any wet market across China.

1斤 (jat1 gan1) is equivalent to 1.1lbs or 500 grams in Mainland China, but 1.3lbs or 600 grams in Hong Kong and Macau. This term might sound strange and unfamiliar to many Western audiences, but yes, it's a real word!

Sample Sentences C

唔該，我要一斤牛肉。

[m4-goi1, ngo5 jiu3 jat1 gan1 ngau4-juk6]

Excuse me, I would like a catty of beef.

一斤豬肉幾錢呀？

[jat1 gan1 zyu1-juk6 gei2-cin2 aa3?]

How much is one catty of pork?

呢度嘅雞肉好貴。

[ni1-dou6 ge3 gai1-juk6 hou2 gwai3]

The chicken here is very expensive.

我買咗半磅叉燒。

[ngo5 maai5 zo2 bun3 bong6 caa1-siu1]

I bought a half pound of roast pork.

| 叉燒 [caa1-siu1] = roast pork; char siu

我想要半斤白菜，唔想要太多。

[ngo5 soeng2 jiu3 bun3 gan1 baak6-coi3, m4 soeng2 jiu3 taai3-do1]

I would like a half catty of bok-choy; I don't want too much.

我今日喺元朗買咗兩斤豬肉。

[ngo5 gam1-jat6 hai2 jyun4-long5 maai5 zo2 loeng5 gan1 zyu1-juk6]

I bought two catties of pork in Yuen Long today.

Recognizing and Writing Chinese Characters

Spoken	Written	Definition	Stroke Order	Word Pair
-	水 [seoi2]	water	丨 刁 水 水	
-	斤 [gan1]	catty	丿 厂 亍 斤	一斤 [jat1 gan1] one catty
-	牛 [ngau4]	ox	丿 𠂉 乞 牛	
-	午 [ng5]	noon	丿 𠂉 乞 午	
-	早 [zou2]	early	丶 冂 曰 日 旦 早	
-	冰 [bing1]	ice	丶 冫 刂 刃 冰 冰	
-	茶 [caa4]	tea	一 十 卄 艹 艾 苓 苶 苶 茶 茶	

Writing Practice

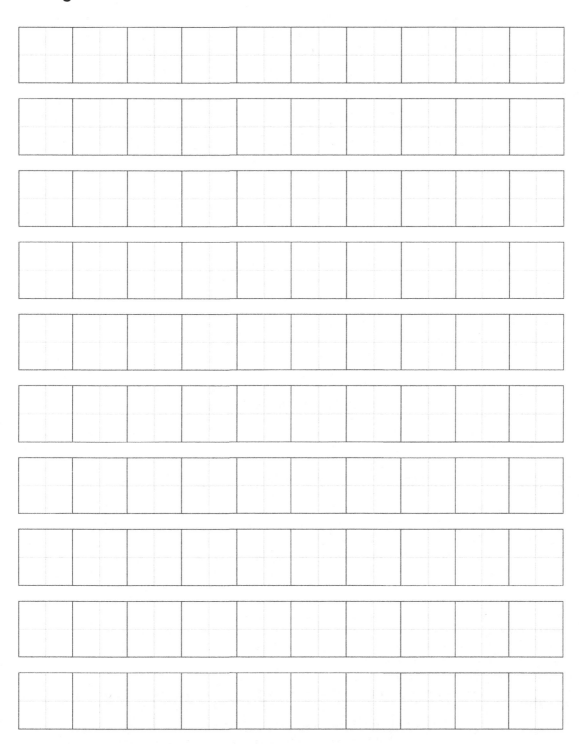

Sample Conversation 🔊

Ben:

你今日午餐想食咩呀？

[nei5 gam1-jat6 ng5-caan1 soeng2 sik6 me1 aa3?]

What would you like to eat for lunch today?

Stormy:

我想食豬扒飯。

[ngo5 soeng2 sik6 zyu1-paa2 faan6]

I want to eat pork chop (with) rice.

Ben:

你想去邊度食呀？

[nei5 soeng2 heoi3 bin1-dou6 sik6 aa3?]

Where do you want to go eat?

Stormy:

茶餐廳啦。

[caa4-caan1-teng1 laa1]

(Let's go to a) Hong Kong-style café restaurant.

Ben:

邊間茶餐廳呀？

[bin1-gaan1 caa4-caan1-teng1 aa3?]

Which Hong Kong-style café restaurant?

Stormy:

我哋屋企附近有間茶餐廳，去嗰度啦。

[ngo5-dei6 uk1-kei2 fu6-gan6 jau5 gaan1 caa4-caan1-teng1, heoi3 go2-dou6 laa1]

There is a Hong Kong-style café near home—let's go there.

Ben:

好呀！[hou2 aa3!]

Sure!

Stormy:

兩位呀，唔該。

[loeng5-wai2 aa3, m4-goi1]

Table for two, please.

Server:

請問你哋想食咩呀？

[cing2-man6 nei5-dei6 soeng2 sik6 me1 aa3?]

May I ask what you would like to eat?

Stormy:

我想要一份豬扒飯。

[ngo5 soeng2 jiu3 jat1-fan6 zyu1-paa2 faan6]

I would like a pork chop (with) rice.

Ben:

我想要一碗牛肉麵走蔥。

[ngo5 soeng2 jiu3 jat1-wun2 ngau4-juk6 min6 zau2 cung1]

I would like a bowl of beef noodles without scallion.

Server:

要唔要飲嘢呀？

[jiu3-m4-jiu3 jam2 je5 aa3?]

Would you like to drink anything?

Ben:

我要一杯咖啡少甜。

[ngo5 jiu3 jat1-bui1 gaa3-fe1 siu2 tim4]

I want a coffee that's less sweet.

Stormy:

我想要一杯奶茶走甜。唔該哂！

[ngo5 soeng2 jiu3 jat1-bui1 naai5-caa4 zau2 tim4. m4-goi1-saai3!]

I would like a milk tea without sugar. Thank you so much!

Cultural Insights | Do people tip in restaurants in Hong Kong?

You are not expected to tip for food service in Hong Kong. Most restaurants in Hong Kong add a 10% service charge automatically to the bill, which is called 加一 (gaa1 jat1) in Cantonese. Because tipping is generally not expected, customers usually take on more responsibilities—for instance, by going up to the counter to pay the bill.

See answers on page #207

Chapter 6 Exercise

1. What is the classifier for restaurants and cafés?

   _____

2. What is the most common mass unit used in China?

   _____

3. What is the final particle that you would use at the end of a sentence to indicate that something is "too ...?"

   _____

4. Translate or transliterate the following sentences:

   [ngo5 soeng2 jiu3 jat1-bui1 naai5-caa4 siu2 tim4]

   我想要一杯奶茶少甜。

   _____

   [nei5 maai5 zo2 jat1-gan1 zyu1-juk6 aa4?]

   你買咗一斤豬肉呀？

   _____

   [loeng5-gan1 ngau4-juk6 taai3 do1 laa3!]

   兩斤牛肉太多喇！

   _____

   [____ ____ ____ ____ ____ ____ laa3!]

   呢杯咖啡太苦喇！

   This cup of coffee is too bitter!

Part II Review: Summer

- To express a contradiction with "although ..., ..." you can say 雖然..., 但係... (seoi1-jin4 ..., daan6-hai6 ...).

- To tell someone your opinion, you can say "我覺得... (ngo5 gok3-dak1 ...) I think ...."

- 喇 (laa3) is a final particle that can be used to indicate a state of change or to express certainty.

- 呀 (aa4) is a final particle that is used to express surprise in a question when it is used in fourth tone.

- The most ... = 最 (zeoi3) + adj.

- Too ... = 太 (taai3) + adj.

- The classifier for rooms is 間 (gaan1)

- To ask how many, you can say 幾多 (gei2-do1)?

- To ask how large, you can say 幾大 (gei2-daai6)?

- To ask for the time, you can use 幾點 (gei2 dim2)?

- Inside = 裏面 (leoi5-min6) | outside = 出面 (ceot1-min6)

- Near = 近 (kan5) | far = 遠 (jyun5)

- To introduce someone to the amenities in the vicinity, you can say 呢度附近有... (ni1-dou6 fu6-gan6 jau5 ...).

See answers on page #208

Sample Paragraph

我想喺佐敦租一個單位。雖然呢個單位好貴，但係好方便。我好鍾意呢度附近有好多茶餐廳。我最鍾意食茶餐廳嘅嘢。呢度返工好近。我覺得呢個單位唔錯。

[ngo5 soeng2 hai2 zo2-deon1 zou1 jat1-go3 daan1-wai2. seoi1-jin4 ni1-go3 daan1-wai2 hou2 gwai3, daan6-hai6 hou2 fong1-bin6. ngo5 hou2 zung1-ji3 ni1-dou6 fu6-gan6 jau5 hou2-do1 caa4-caan1-teng1. ngo5 zeoi3 zung1-ji3 sik6 caa4-caan1-teng1 ge3 je5. ni1-dou6 faan1-gung1 hou2 kan5. ngo5 gok3-dak1 ni1-go3 daan1-wai2 m4 co3]

I want to rent an apartment unit in Jordan. Although this unit is very expensive, it is very convenient. I like that there are many Hong Kong-style café restaurants near here. I like the food from Hong-Kong style café restaurants the most. Work is very close to here. I think this apartment unit is not bad.

Sample Exercise

Translate or transliterate the following sentences.

1. I think this (apartment) unit is very good.

    [____ ____ ____ ____ ____ ____ ____ ____ ____]

2. [ni1-gaan1 uk1 jau5 jat1-cin1 ping4-fong1 cek3]

    呢間屋有一千平方呎。

    _____

3. You are too kind!

    [____ ____ ____ ____ ____!]

Chapter 7

I go to work at 9AM

我朝早9點返工

As a polar bear who can evolve and adapt quickly to surroundings, I had already developed a balanced work-life schedule by July. In this chapter, I will teach you how to tell time in Cantonese, as well as how to incorporate telling time into daily routines.

After reading this chapter, you should be able to tell someone your daily routine along with the time and the day in relation to the present.

Now, let's take a look at how you can state the time:

number + 點 [dim2] = ... o'clock

10 [sap6] + 點 [dim2] = 10 o'clock

number + 分 [fan1] = ... minute

10點 [sap6 dim2] + 05 [ling4 ng5] + 分 [fan1] = 10:05

10點 [sap6 dim2] + 14 [sap6-sei3] + 分 [fan1] = 10:14

半 [bun3] = half

10點 [sap6 dim2] + 半 [bun3] = 10:30

Vocabulary A 🔊

起身 [hei2-san1] = to get up

刷牙 [caat3 ngaa4] = to brush one's teeth

洗面 [sai2 min6] = to wash one's face

食早餐 [sik6 zou2-caan1] = to eat breakfast

搭車 [daap3 ce1] = to ride a vehicle

返工 [faan1-gung1] = to go to work

食晏 [sik6 aan3] = to eat lunch

收工 [sau1-gung1] = to get off from work

食晚餐 [sik6 maan5-caan1] = to eat dinner

沖涼 [cung1-loeng4] = to take a shower

瞓覺 [fan3-gaau3] = to sleep; to go to bed

休息 [jau1-sik1] = to rest; also indicates days off from work

Sample Sentences A 🔊

我7點起身。

[ngo5 cat1 dim2 hei2-san1]

I get up at 7 o'clock.

然後刷牙洗面。

[jin4-hau6 caat3 ngaa4 sai2 min6]

Then (I) brush my teeth and wash my face.

我8點15分返工。

[ngo5 baat3 dim2 sap6-ng5 fan1 faan1-gung1]

I go to work at 8:15.

你幾點食晏呀？

[nei5 gei2-dim2 sik6 aan3 aa3?]

What time do you eat lunch?

To ask what time it is now, you can use 幾點 (gei2 dim2), which literally means "how many o'clock."

我鍾意喺公司附近食晏。

[ngo5 zung1-ji3 hai2 gung1-si1 fu6-gan6 sik6 aan3]

I like to eat lunch near (my) company.

我10點半瞓覺。

[ngo5 sap6 dim2 bun3 fan3-gaau3]

I go to bed at 10:30.

我10點30分瞓覺。

[ngo5 sap6 dim2 saam1-sap6 fan1 fan3-gaau3]

I go to bed at 10:30.

As you can see, there are at least two ways to express the time as 10:30.

Vocabulary B 🔊

朝早 [ziu1-zou2] = morning

晏晝 [aan3-zau3] = noon; afternoon

下晝 [haa6-zau3] = afternoon

夜晚 [je6-maan5] = night

而家 [ji4-gaa1] = now

頭先 [tau4-sin1] = just now; before

一陣間 [jat1-zan6-gaan1] = later

To greet someone with "good morning," you say "早晨 (zou2-san4)" instead of "朝早 (ziu1-zou2)."

Sentence Structure Takeaway

而家 [ji4-gaa1] + number + 點 [dim2] = It's … o'clock now

而家 [ji4-gaa1] + 幾 [gei2] + 點 [dim2]? = What time is it now?*

*Literal meaning: now what time?

Sample Sentences B 🔊

而家係11點57分。

[ji4-gaa1 hai6 sap6-jat1 dim2 ng5-sap6-cat1 fan1]

It's 11:57 now.

而家幾點呀？

[ji4-gaa1 gei2-dim2 aa3?]

What time is it now?

而家9點20分喇！

[ji4-gaa1 gau2 dim2 ji6-sap6 fan1 laa3!]

It's 9:20 now!

This is the third time we are introducing the final particle 喇 (laa3) in this book. 喇 (laa3) can be also used to express a transition in time period, or some other state of change. Here, it is used for both purposes: "It's already 9:20, (and something needs to be done)."

我朝早6點半起身。

[ngo5 ziu1-zou2 luk6 dim2 bun3 hei2-san1]

I wake up at 6:30AM.

我下晝3點要飲咖啡。

[ngo5 haa6-zau3 saam1 dim2 jiu3 jam2 gaa3-fe1]

I have to drink coffee at 3 o'clock in the afternoon.

In basic Chinese sentence structure, you always place the time before the verb.

我哋一陣間7點45分見！

[ngo5-dei6 jat1-zan6-gaan1 cat1 dim2 sei3-sap6-ng5 fan1 gin3!]

We will see each other later at 7:45!

點解你夜晚8點要返工？

[dim2-gaai2 nei5 je6-maan5 baat3 dim2 jiu3 faan1-gung1?]

Why do you need to work at 8PM?

你而家做緊咩呀？

[nei5 ji4-gaa1 zou6 gan2 me1 aa3?]

What are you doing now?

你一陣間要做咩呀？

[nei5 jat1-zan6-gaan1 jiu3 zou6 me1 aa3?]

What do you have to do later?

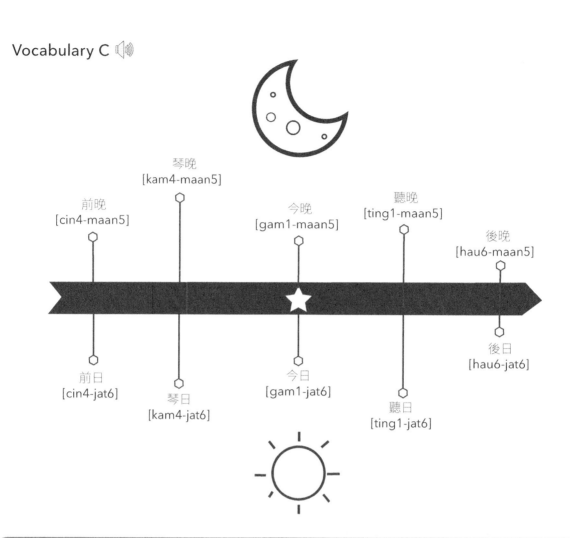

前晚
[cin4-maan5]

琴晚
[kam4-maan5]

今晚
[gam1-maan5]

聽晚
[ting1-maan5]

後晚
[hau6-maan5]

前日
[cin4-jat6]

琴日
[kam4-jat6]

今日
[gam1-jat6]

聽日
[ting1-jat6]

後日
[hau6-jat6]

日 [jat6] = day

晚 [maan5] = night

前日 [cin4-jat6] = the day before yesterday

前晚 [cin4-maan5] = the night before last night

琴日 [kam4-jat6] = yesterday

琴晚 [kam4-maan5] = last night

今日 [gam1-jat6] = today

今晚 [gam1-maan5] = tonight

聽日 [ting1-jat6] = tomorrow

聽晚 [ting1-maan5] = tomorrow night

後日 [hau6-jat6] = the day after tomorrow

後晚 [hau6-maan5] = the night after tomorrow's night

Sample Sentences C 🔊

你琴晚去咗邊度呀？

[nei5 kam4-maan5 heoi3 zo2 bin1-dou6 aa3?]

Where did you go last night?

我前晚10點瞓咗。

[ngo5 cin4-maan5 sap6 dim2 fan3 zo2]

I slept at 10PM the night before last night.

你琴晚幾點沖涼呀？

[nei5 kam4-maan5 gei2 dim2 cung1-loeng4 aa3?]

What time did you shower last night?

我今晚唔去好好餐廳食晚餐。

[ngo5 gam1-maan5 m4 heoi3 hou2-hou2 caan1-teng1 sik6 maan5-caan1]

I am not going to Hou Hou Restaurant to eat dinner tonight.

點解佢今日唔去呀？

[dim2-gaai2 keoi5 gam1-jat6 m4 heoi3 aa3?]

Why is he not going today?

陳大明先生琴日10點20分返咗工。

[can4-daai6-ming4 sin1-saang1 kam4-jat6 sap6 dim2 ji6-sap6 fan1 faan1 zo2 gung1]

Mr. Tai Ming Chan went to work at 10:20 yesterday.

我想你聽日9點半嚟。

[ngo5 soeng2 nei5 ting1-jat6 gau2 dim2 bun3 lei4]

I want you to come (here) at 9:30 tomorrow.

Recognizing and Writing Characters

Spoken	Written	Definition	Stroke Order	Word Pair
	工 [gung1]	job	一 丁 工	
	日 [jat6]	day	丨 冂 日 日	
	分 [fan1]	minute; point; to split	丿 八 分 分	分鐘 [fan-zung1] minute
	牙 [ngaa4]	tooth	一 二 于 牙	
	字 [zi6]	character	丶 丷 宀 宀 字 字	
吃 [hek3]	食 [sik6]	to eat	丨 冂 口 口 吃 吃	
	明 [ming4]	understand; clear; Ming Dynasty	丨 冂 月 日 刖 明 明 明	

Writing Practice

Sample Conversation 🔊

Stormy:

Ben, 起身喇！[hei2-san1 laa3]

Ben, it's time to get up!

Review Sample Sentences B to refresh the usage of the final particle 喇 (laa3).

Ben:

Stormy, 而家幾點呀？

[Stormy, ji4-gaa1 gei2 dim2 aa3?]

Stormy, what time is it now?

Stormy:

7點半喇！

[cat1 dim2 bun3 laa3!]

It's 7:30!

Ben:

吓？我要返工喇！

[haa2? ngo5 jiu3 faan1-gung1 laa3!]

Huh? I have to go to work!

Stormy:

你去刷牙洗面啦！你食唔食早餐呀？

[nei5 heoi3 caat3 ngaa4 sai2 min6 laa1! nei5
sik6-m4-sik6 zou2-caan1 aa3?]

Go brush your teeth and wash your face!
Are you going to eat breakfast?

Ben:

唔食喇。[m4 sik6 laa3]

No, not eating.

Stormy:

你去邊度食早餐呀？

[nei5 heoi3 bin1-dou6 sik6 zou2-caan1 aa3?]

Where are you going to eat breakfast?

Ben:

我一陣間喺學校食。

[ngo5 jat1-zan6-gaan1 hai2 hok6-haau6 sik6]

I (will) eat later at school.

Stormy:

好啦，今晚見。[hou2 laa1, gam1-maan5 gin3]

Okay, see you tonight.

Ben:

拜拜。[baai1-baai3]

Bye.

Cultural Insights | Using 個字 (go3 zi6) to express the increment of five minutes

Telling time in Cantonese can be very different than in English especially when it is in the increment of five minutes. Every five minutes is considered 1個字(jat1-go3 zi6). For example:

1個字 [jat1-go3 zi6] = 5 minute

10點 [sap6-dim2] + 1個字 [jat1-go3 zi6] = 10:05

10點 [sap6-dim2] + 4個字 [sei3-go3 zi6] = 10:20

Think about when you are visually reading the clock, "…個字 (go3 zi6)" simply comes from the number where the minutes hand is pointing. Take a look at the following examples:

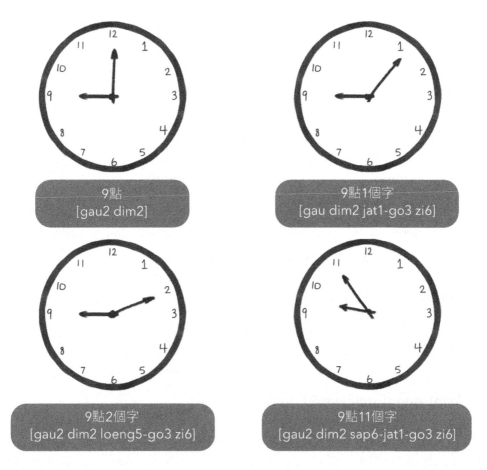

9點
[gau2 dim2]

9點1個字
[gau dim2 jat1-go3 zi6]

9點2個字
[gau2 dim2 loeng5-go3 zi6]

9點11個字
[gau2 dim2 sap6-jat1-go3 zi6]

See answers on page #208

Chapter 7 Exercises

1. How do you express "... o'clock" in Cantonese?

   _____

2. What are the two ways to express the time 4:30?

   _____

3. What is the interrogative word (question word) you use to ask someone, "What time is it?"

   _____

4. Draw a line to connect the appropriate Chinese words to its translation:

   食晏 [sik6 aan3]   later

   休息 [jau1-sik1]   to rest

   瞓覺 [fan3-gaau3]   tomorrow night

   一陣間 [jat1-zan6-gaan1]   to eat lunch

   聽晚 [ting1-maan5]   to go to

   去 [heoi3]   to sleep

5. Translate or transliterate the following sentences:

   [nei5 gei2 dim2 faan1-gung1 aa3?]

   你幾點返工呀?

   _____

   [nei5 faan1-gung1 gei2 dim2 hei2-san1 aa3?]

   你返工幾點起身呀?

   _____

我一陣間去你屋企。

I will go to your home later.

_____

[ngo5 kam4-maan5 sap6-ji6 dim2 bun3 fan3-gaau3]

我琴晚12點半瞓覺。

_____

6. Transliterate the following times:

7:44 _____

8:56 _____

9:13 _____

2:10 _____

Why don't we go …?

不如我哋去…啦

Since August marks the hottest month of the summer in Hong Kong, Stormy and I started exploring fun activities in the city. At a speed dating event, we learned how to discuss our favorite pastimes in hopes of finding a soulmate who loves nature as much as we do. In this chapter, you will learn the names of various activities in Cantonese, along with the frequency of practice. You will also get more exposure to telling time and applying it to activities. After reading this chapter, you will be able to share your hobbies and how often you engage in them.

不如我哋 [bat1-jyu4 ngo5-dei6] + 去 [heoi3] + activity + 啦 [laa1] = why don't we go …

不如我哋 [bat1-jyu4 ngo5-dei6] + 去 [heoi3] + 食嘢 [sik6 je5] + 啦 [laa1] = why don't we go eat

In Chapter 3, we learned that the final particle 啦 (laa1) is often used at the end of an imperative sentence as a command or suggestion.

Vocabulary A 🔊

聽音樂 [teng1 jam1-ngok6] = to listen to music

行街 [haang4-gaai1] = to go shopping

睇戲 [tai2 hei3] = to see a movie

睇書 [tai2 syu1] = to read

唱K [coeng3-kei1] = to do karaoke

影相 [jing2-soeng2] = to take photos

游水 [jau4-seoi2] = to swim

行山 [haang4-saan1] = to hike

睇演唱會 [tai2 jin2-coeng3 wui2] = to see a concert

睇棟篤笑 [tai2 dung6-duk1 siu3] = to see a standup comedy show

Sample Sentences A 🔊

我禮拜六去行山。

[ngo5 lai5-baai3-luk6 heoi3 haang4-saan1]

I go hiking on Saturdays.

我星期六去咗行山。

[ngo5 sing1-kei4-luk6 heoi3 zo2 haang4-saan1]

I went hiking on Saturday.

Remember we learned in Book 1 that "禮拜 (lai5-baai3)" means "week?" In this book, we will use "禮拜 (lai5-baai3)" and "星期 (sing1-kei4)" interchangeably because they both mean "week."

不如我哋星期六去行山啦！

[bat1-jyu4 ngo5-dei6 sing1-kei4-luk6 heoi3 haang4-saan1 laa1!]

Why don't we go hiking on Saturday?

聽日係星期二，不如我哋去睇戲啦！

[ting1-jat6 hai6 sing1-kei4-ji6, bat1-jyu4 ngo5-dei6 heoi3 tai2 hei3 laa1!]

Tomorrow is Tuesday; why don't we go see a movie?

我鍾意聽音樂。

[ngo5 zung1-ji3 teng1 jam1-ngok6]

I like to listen to music.

你想唔想去唱K呀？

[nei5 soeng2-m4-soeng2 heoi3 coeng3-kei1 aa3?]

Do you want to go do karaoke?

7月我鍾意去游水。

[cat1-jyut6 ngo5 zung1-ji3 heoi3 jau4-seoi2]

I like to go swimming in July.

第一，我哋去行街，然後去睇戲。

[dai6-jat1, ngo5-dei6 heoi3 haang4-gaai1, jin4-hau6 heoi3 tai2 hei3]

First, we (will) go shopping, and then we will go see a movie.

Vocabulary B 🔊

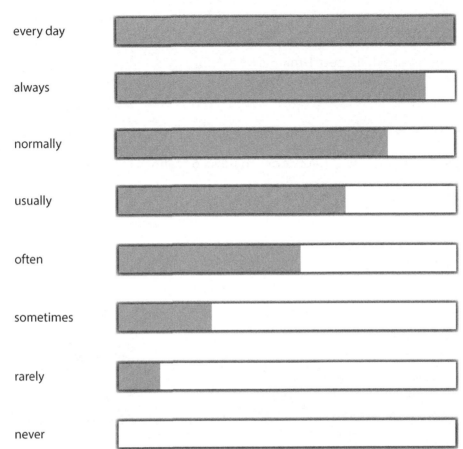

every day

always

normally

usually

often

sometimes

rarely

never

每日 [mui5-jat6] = every day

成日 [seng4-jat6] = always

平時 [ping4-si4] = normally

通常 [tung1-soeng4] = usually

經常 [ging1-soeng4] = often

有時 [jau5-si4] = sometimes

好少 [hou2-siu2] = rarely

冇…過 [mou5 … gwo3] = have never done…

Sample Sentences B 🔊

佢哋成日喺出面食飯。

[keoi5-dei6 seng4-jat6 hai2 ceot1-min6 sik6 faan6]

They always go out to eat.

我屋企人好少喺出面食飯。

[ngo5 uk1-kei5 jan4 hou2-siu2 hai2 ceot1-min6 sik6 faan6]

My family rarely goes out to eat.

我每日都睇中文書。

[ngo5 mui5-jat6 dou1 tai2 zung3-man2 syu1]

I read Chinese books every day.

When 每日 (mui5-jat6) is used, 都 (dou1) is often added after it to emphasize "every day without exception."

我平時鍾意去嗰度影相。

[ngo5 ping4-si4 zung1-ji3 heoi3 go2-dou6 jing2-soeng2]

I normally like to go there to take photos.

你通常去邊度行山呀?

[nei5 tung1-soeng4 heoi3 bin1-dou6 haang4-saan1 aa3?]

Where do you usually like to hike?

你通常幾點收工呀？

[nei5 tung1-soeng4 gei2-dim2 sau1-gung1 aa3?]

What time do you usually get off work?

你成日係噉！

[nei5 seng4-jat6 hai6 gam2!]

You are always like that!

我冇去過。[ngo5 mou5 heoi3 gwo3]

I have never been there.

我冇去過嗰度唱K。

[ngo5 mou5 heoi3 gwo3 go2-dou6 coeng3-kei1]

I have never been there for karaoke.

我冇睇過廣東話嘅棟篤笑。

[ngo5 mou5 tai2 gwo3 gwong2-dung1 waa2 ge3 dung6-duk1 siu3]

I have never seen a Cantonese standup comedy show.

Now that you can express how frequently you engage in your favorite activity, let's learn some new verbs and refresh your memory of some old ones so that you can add more details to your sentences.

Vocabulary C 🔊

嚟 [lei4] = to come

去 [heoi3] = to go to

走 [zau2] = 1 to leave; 2 to walk

知 [zi1] = to know (information)

識 [sik1] = to know (person or skill)

Remember this is the same character "走 (zau2)" from "走甜 (zau2 tim4) less sweet" in Chapter 6?

玩 [waan2] = 1 to play; 2 to hang out

參加 [caam1-gaa1] = to attend

邀請 [jiu1-cing2] = to invite

請 [ceng2] = to treat

As you may have noticed, the character 請 (cing2/ceng2) is the same in both "to invite" and "to treat", but with different pronunciations. This is called a heteronym; the same word can have different meanings when it is pronounced differently. For example, "present" in English can be pronounced differently to mean "a gift" or "to formally introduce."

Sample Sentences C 🔊

你想幾點走？[nei5 soeng2 gei2-dim2 zau2?]

What time do you want to leave?

佢邀請咗邊個呀？

[keoi5 jiu1-cing2 zo2 bin1-go3 aa3?]

Who did he invite?

今日我請食飯。[gam1-jat6 ngo5 ceng2 sik6 faan6]

I am treating (you) to the meal today.

佢琴日請我睇戲。

[keoi5 kam4-jat6 ceng2 ngo5 tai2 hei3]

He/she treated me to a movie yesterday.

我鍾意行山多過游水。

[ngo5 zung1-ji3 haang4-saan1 do1-gwo3 jau4-seoi2]

I like hiking more than swimming.

Grammar Takeaway

多啲 [do1-di1] = more

多過 [do1-gwo3] = more than

A多啲 [A do1-di1] = A is more

A多過B [A do1-gwo3 B] = A is more than B

鍾意A多啲 [zung1-ji3 A do1-di1] = to like A more

鍾意A多過B [zung1-ji3 A do1-gwo3 B] = to like A more than B

呢本書好過嗰本書。

[ni1-bun2 syu1 hou2 gwo3 go2-bun2 syu1]

This book is better than that book.

我阿媽煮嘅豆腐好味啲。

[ngo5 aa3-maa1 zyu2 ge3 dau6-fu6 hou2-mei6 di1]

The tofu that my mom cooks is more delicious.

我鍾意屋企附近嘅咖啡店多啲。

[ngo5 zung1-ji3 uk1-kei2 fu6-gan6 ge3 gaa3-fe1 dim3 do1-di1]

I like the café near home more.

| 咖啡店 [gaa3-fe1 dim3] = café

Recognizing and Writing Chinese Characters

Spoken	Written	Definition	Stroke Order						Word Pair
-	上 [soeng2/ soeng6]	top	丨	上	上				
-	下 [haa6]	bottom	一	丁	下				
-	山 [saan1]	mountain	丨	山	山				
-	少 [siu2]	few	丨	小	小	少			
-	去 [heoi3]	to go	一	十	土	去	去		
-	多 [do1]	many	丿	勹	夕	多	多	多	
冇 [mou5]	沒 [mut6]	to not have	丶	丶	氵	汈	汈	沒	沒有 [mut6-jau5] to not have

Writing Practice

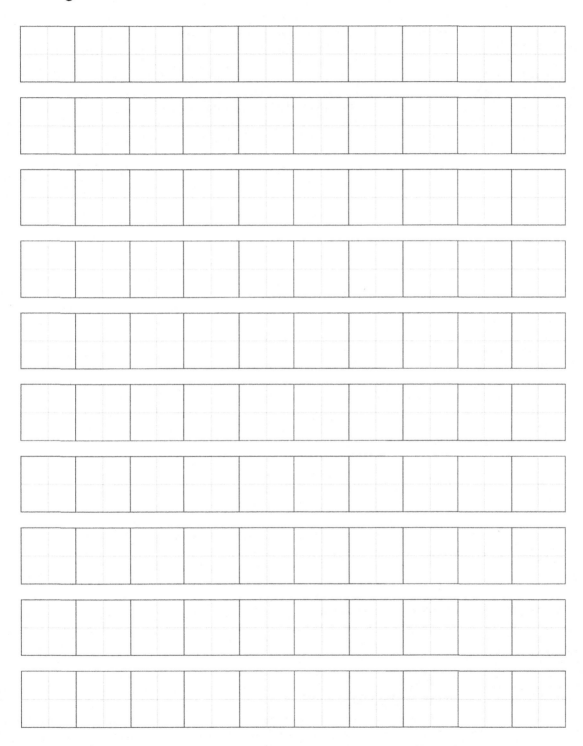

Sample Conversation 🔊

Stormy:

你好，你叫咩名呀？

[nei5-hou2, nei5 giu3 me1 meng2 aa3?]

Hi, what is your name?

Meow-Meow:

我叫喵喵。

[ngo5 giu3 meu1-meu1]

My name is Meow-Meow.

Stormy:

你平時禮拜日鍾意做咩呀？

[nei5 ping4-si4 lai5-baai3-jat6 zung1-ji3 zou6 me1 aa3?]

What do you usually like to do on Sundays?

Meow-Meow:

我鍾意行山同睇戲。

[ngo5 zung1-ji3 haang4-saan1 tung4 tai2 hei3]

I like to hike and watch movies.

Stormy:

係呀？我都好鍾意行山同睇戲。

[hai6 aa4? ngo5 dou1 hou2 zung1-ji3 haang4-saan1 tung4 tai2 hei3]

Really? I also like hiking and watching movies.

你最鍾意去邊度行山呀？

[nei5 zeoi3 zung1-ji3 heoi3 bin1-dou6 haang4-saan1 aa3?]

Where do you like to go hiking?

Meow-Meow:

我最鍾意去獅子山，你呢？

[ngo5 zeoi3 zung1-ji3 heoi3 si1-zi2 saan1, nei5 ne1?]

I like to go to Lion Rock the most, (and) what about you?

Stormy:

我鍾意去大帽山多啲。

[ngo5 zung1-ji3 heoi3 daai6-mou6 saan1 do1-di1]

I like to go to Tai Mo Shan more.

Meow-Meow:

我冇去過大帽山。

[ngo5 mou5 heoi3 gwo3 daai6-mou6 saan1]

I have never been to Tai Mo Shan.

Stormy:

不如我哋下個禮拜日一齊去大帽山啦！

[bat1-jyu4 ngo5-dei6 haa6-go3 lai5-baai3-jat6 jat1-cai4 heoi3 daai6-mou6-saan1 laa1!]

Why don't we go together to Tai Mo Shan next Sunday?

| 一齊 [jat1-cai4] = together

Meow-Meow:

好呀。

[hou2 aa3]

That sounds good.

Cultural Insights | Fighting over the check

This is what you may encounter when you eat out with a Chinese friend: when the check comes, your friend offers to pay even though it is not a special day or celebration. What does that mean and why is this friend offering to treat you on a day that is not a special occasion?

In the Chinese culture, food is considered the source of life. There is even an idiom that says 民以食為天 (man4 ji5 sik6 wai4 tin1), which means people regard food as their heaven. Therefore, treating others to a meal means much more than simply offering the food itself, but also establishing a valuable relationship with them. It is considered a courtesy and privilege to treat others, rather than a ceremony for special events.

In practice, one always "fights back" to get the check to express gratitude and courtesy when the other person offers to pay. The "fight" can go back and forth, because it is considered impolite if you let the other person pay on his first attempt. The relationship is often reciprocal: when one person treats another person to one meal, the other person usually treats him to the next one.

See answers on page #209

Chapter 8 Exercises

1. What is the word that you use to compare when A is "more than" B?

   _____

2. How can you suggest an activity to your friend by saying, "Why don't we …?"

   _____

3. What does 山 (saan1) mean in 行山 (haang4-saan1)?

   _____

4. How do you express, "I've never …?"

   _____

5. What is the word that is used after "every day" when you try to express "every time without exception?"

   _____

6. Translate or transliterate the following sentences:

   [____ ____ ____ ____ ____ ____ ____]

   我平時鍾意睇書。

   I normally like to read.

   [nei5 lai5-baai3-jat6 tung1-soeng4 zou6 me1 aa3?]

   你禮拜日通常做咩呀？

   _____

[___ ___ ___ ___ ___ ___ ___ ___ ___]

我鍾意行山多過行街。

I like hiking more than shopping.

Chapter 9

I Wear A Size Medium Shirt

我著中碼衫

Many locals refer to Hong Kong as a "Shopping Paradise" as it is famous for being a fashion, cosmetics, and jewelry hub. In this chapter, I will introduce you to Cantonese names for each piece of clothing and its corresponding classifier. More importantly, I will teach you how to apply them in real-life scenarios when you are shopping. In addition, we will also explore how to choose sizes using Cantonese. After reading this chapter, you will be able to shop at any places in Hong Kong, and even negotiate prices at a local retail store.

Vocabulary A 🔊

衫 [saam1] = shirt; garment

短袖衫 [dyun2-zau6 saam1] = short sleeve clothing

長袖衫 [coeng4-zau6 saam1] = long sleeve clothing

冷衫 [laang1-saam1] = sweater

外套 [ngoi6-tou3] = coat

背心 [bui3-sam1] = vest; tank top

褲 [fu3] = pants; trousers

長褲 [coeng4 fu3] = pants

短褲 [dyun2 fu3] = shorts

牛仔褲 [ngau4-zai2-fu3] = jeans

裙 [kwan4] = dress

底衫 [dai2-saam1] = underwear

底褲 [dai2-fu3] = panties

Sample Sentences A 🔊

我想買一件短袖衫。

[ngo5 soeng2 maai5 jat1-gin6 dyun2-zau6 saam1]

I want to buy a t-shirt.

| 件 (gin6) is the classifier for tops

我鍾意呢條褲。

[ngo5 zung1-ji3 ni1-tiu4 fu3]

I like this (pair of) pants.

| 條 (tiu4) is the classifier for bottoms

呢條裙好靚呀 ![ni1-tiu4 kwan4 hou2 leng3 aa3!]

This dress is very pretty!

| 靚 [leng3] = pretty; good-quality

你屋企有冇長袖衫呀？

[nei5 uk1-kei2 jau5-mou5 coeng4-zau6 saam1 aa3?]

Do you have a long sleeve shirt at home?

呢度有好多好靚嘅牛仔褲。

[ni1-dou6 jau5 hou2 do1 hou2 leng3 ge3 ngau4-zai2-fu3]

There are many good-quality jeans here.

Vocabulary B 🔊

碼 [maa5] = size

大碼 [daai6 maa5] = large size

加大碼 [gaa1 daai6 maa5] = extra-large size

加加大碼 [gaa1 gaa1 daai6 maa5] = extra extra-large size

中碼 [zung1 maa5] = medium size

細碼 [sai3 maa5] = small size

加細碼 [gaa1 sai3 maa5] = extra-small size

著 [zoek3] = to wear

試 [si3] = to try

新 [san1] = new

舊 [gau6] = old (for objects)

平 [peng4] = inexpensive

貴 [gwai3] = expensive

Sample Sentences B 🔊

你有冇加大碼呀？

[nei5 jau5-mou5 gaa1-daai6 maa5 aa3?]

Do you have a size extra-large?

我著細碼。

[ngo5 zoek3 sai3 maa5]

I wear a size small.

呢件衫太大喇，有冇中碼呀？

[ni1-gin6 saam1 taai3 daai6 laa3, jau5-mou5 zung1 maa5 aa3?]

This shirt is too large, is there a size medium?

邊度可以試衫呀？

[bin1-dou6 ho2-ji5 si3 saam1 aa3?]

Where can I try on the clothes?

Remember, the final particle 喇 (laa3) is added when "太 (taai3) too..." is used to express excessiveness.

我想試著呢件衫。

[ngo5 soeng2 si3 zoek3 ni1-gin6 saam1]

I want to try this shirt on.

呢件衫你有冇新嘅？

[ni1-gin6 saam1 nei5 jau5-mou5 san1 ge3?]

Do you have any more of these shirts?

In this example, 衫 (saam1) is omitted after "新嘅 (san1-ge3)" because it is already mentioned once earlier.

我著24碼嘅牛仔褲。

[ngo5 zoek3 ji6-sap6-sei3 maa5 ge3 ngau4-zai2-fu3]

I wear size 24 jeans.

我唔知我著咩碼。

[ngo5 m4 zi1 ngo5 zoek3 me1 maa5]

I don't know what size I wear.

Vocabulary C 🔊

襪 [mat6] = socks

鞋 [haai4] = shoes

波鞋 [bo1-haai4] = sneakers

涼鞋 [loeng4-haai4] = sandals

平底鞋 [ping4-dai2-haai4] = flats

皮鞋 [pei4-haai4] = leather shoes

靴 [hoe1] = boots

Sample Sentences C 🔊

我著37號嘅鞋。

[ngo5 zoek3 saam1-sap6-cat1 hou6 ge3 haai4]

I wear a size 37 shoe.

In Book 1, we learned that 號 (hou6) is used to represent numbers, for example, 4號 (sei3 hou6) for "number 4."

佢著8號半嘅鞋呀？

[keoi5 zoek3 baat3 hou6 bun3 ge3 haai4 aa4?]

He wears a size 8.5 shoe?

| 半 [bun3] = half

你想買咩鞋呀？

[nei5 soeng2 maai5 me1 haai4 aa3?]

What shoes do you want to buy?

我想買一對返工嘅鞋。

[ngo5 soeng2 maai5 jat1-deoi3 faan1-gung1 ge3 haai4]

I want to buy a pair of work shoes.

| 一對 [jat1-deoi3] = one pair

呢對襪好舊喇！

[ni1-deoi3 mat6 hou2 gau6 laa3]

This pair of socks is very old!

Recognizing and Writing Chinese Characters

Spoken	Written	Definition	Stroke Order					Word Pair
細 [sai3]	小 [siu2]	small	亅	亅	小			
-	中 [zung1]	medium; middle	丨	冂	口	中		
-	以 [ji5]	by means of	㇄	㇄	㠯	以		可以 [ho2-i5] can
-	可 [ho2]	can	一	丁	刁	可	可	
-	加 [gaa1]	plus	㇆	力	加	加	加	
-	件 [gin6]	piece	丿	亻	亻	仵	件	一件 [jat1-gin6] one piece of top clothing
衫 [saam1]	衣 [ji1]	shirt	丶	一	亣	龙	衣	

Writing Practice

Sample Conversation

Ben:

你好，請問背心喺邊度呀？

[nei5-hou2, cing2-man6 bui3-sam1 hai2 bin1-dou6 aa3?]

Hi, where are the tank tops please?

Salesperson:

背心喺呢度。[bui3-sam1 hai2 ni1-dou6]

The tank tops are here.

Ben:

有冇白色加大碼呀？

[jau5-mou5 baak6-sik1 gaa1-daai6 maa5 aa3?]

Is there a size extra-large in white?

Salesperson:

冇白色，但係有灰色同黑色。

[mou5 baak6-sik1, daan6-hai6 jau5 fui1-sik1 tung4 hak1-sik1]

There's no white, but there's gray and black.

Ben:

Stormy, 你覺得邊個顏色好啲呀？

[Stormy, nei5 gok3-dak1 bin1-go3 ngaan4-sik1 hou2-di1 aa3?]

Stormy, which color do you think is better?

Stormy:

我覺得灰色好啲。

[ngo5 gok3-dak1 fui1-sik1 hou2-di1]

I think gray is better.

Ben:

請問邊度可以試衫呀?

[cing2-man6 bin1-dou6 ho2-ji5 si3 saam1 aa3?]

Where can I try on the clothes please?

Salesperson:

試衣室喺嗰度。

[si3 ji1 sat1 hai2 go2-dou6]

The fitting room is over there.

| 試衣室 [si3 ji1 sat1] = fitting room

Ben:

唔該。[m4-goi1]

Thank you.

Cultural Insights | Bargaining in Hong Kong

Bargaining is not appropriate everywhere in Hong Kong, such as department stores, chains, and supermarkets. However, it is acceptable in most family-owned stores and in markets, such as Temple Street Night Market and Apliu Street Flea Market. Bargaining is a survival skill in China. For small retail vendors, some prices are marked higher than market price so that you are expected to bargain for a lower amount than the offered price. Think of it as one of the beauties of experiencing a different culture, and also a chance for you to practice your Cantonese with locals. Plus, you will find very good deals!

What can you bargain for?

- Cars

- Clothes

- Furniture

- Groceries in the market

- Electronics

How do you bargain the price of a sweater listed as $60?

1. After you learn about the price, give a price that is lower than what you expect to pay. For example, depending on the quality of the sweater, if you would like to get it for $50, ask for $40.

   60蚊太貴喇。40蚊得唔得？

   [luk6-sap6 man1 taai3 gwai3 laa3. sei3-sap6 man1 dak1-m4-dak1?]

   $60 is too expensive. Is $40 okay?

2.   Mention the flaws of the sweater that you can see, for example, it is not warm enough for winters, or the color of the sweater is very hard to match with other clothes.

呢件冷衫麻麻哋。

[ni1-gin6 laang1-saam1 maa4-maa2-dei2]

This sweater is so-so.

3.   If the lowest price offered is $55 after bargaining back and forth and you are still not satisfied, try leaving the store. (Your closet is probably full of other treasures anyway!)

算啦，唔買喇。[syun3 laa1, m4 maai5 laa3]

Never mind, I am not buying anymore.

But note that if this is something that you think is the deal of a lifetime, take it for $55 and know that you already used your opportunity to practice Cantonese and also got a $5 discount.

See answers on page #209

Chapter 9 Exercises

1. What do you add before the adjective to express "too much ...?"

    _____

2. What is the classifier for tops?

    _____

3. What is the classifier for bottoms?

    _____

4. What is the generic word for clothes?

    _____

5. Translate the following sentences:

    [ngo5 soeng2 jiu3 jat1-deoi3 bo1-haai4]

    我想要一對波鞋。

    _____

    [jau5-mou5 saam1-sap6-cat1 hou6 bun3?]

    有冇37號半？

    _____

    [___ ___ ___ ___ ___ ___ ___ ___]

    我想試著呢件冷衫。

    I would like to try this sweater on.

[___ ___ ___ ___ ___]

呢對鞋太細。

This pair of shoes is too small.

6.   Translate the following sizes:

XL   加大碼 [___ ___ maa5]

S   細碼 [___ maa5]

M   中碼 [___ maa5]

Size 34   34號 [___ ___ ___ hou6]

Size 8.5   8號半 [___ ___ ___]

Part III Review: Autumn

- To state the exact time, you can add the hour + 點 (dim2) and minute + 分 (fan1).

- Applying the subject-verb-object sentence structure in Chinese, you always place the time before the verb.

- To make a suggestion to your friends, you can say, "不如我哋…啦 (bat1-jyu4 ngo5-dei6 … laa1) why don't we …?"

- The final particle 啦 (laa1) is used to show a command or suggestion.

- 都 (dou1) is often added after "every day" and before the verb to emphasize "every time without exception."

- To tell someone that you have never done something, you can say, "我冇…過 (ngo5 mou5 … gwo3)."

- To tell someone that you are treating or paying for them, you can say, "我請 (ngo5 ceng2) I am treating."

- 多 (do1) means "more," and 少 (siu2) means "less"

- A is more than B = A 多過 B (A do1-gwo3 B)

- A is more = A 多啲 (A do1-di1)

- 食晏 (sik6 aan3) is a casual way of saying "to eat lunch."

- To show your politeness when you are asking a question formally, you can add "請問 (cing2-man6) may I ask" before you ask your question.

- To tell someone your clothing size, you can add "碼 (maa5)" after the number.

- To tell someone your shoe size, you can add "號 (hou6)" after the number.

- The classifier for tops is 件 (gin6).

See answers on page #210

- The classifier for bottoms is 條 (tiu4).

- 對 (deoi3) means "a pair," but it is not used for pants or shorts.

Sample Paragraphs

我好鍾意Amy。我想請佢食飯。佢鍾意食意大利菜多過美國菜。

[ngo5 hou2 zung1-ji3 Amy. ngo5 soeng2 ceng2 keoi5 sik6 faan6. keoi5 zung1-ji3 sik6 ji3-daai6-lei6 coi3 do1-gwo3 mei5-gwok3 coi3]

I really like Amy. I want to treat her to a meal. She likes to eat Italian food more than American food.

我唔知著咩衫。不如我著灰色嘅冷衫啦？

[ngo5 m4 zi1 zoek3 me1 saam1. bat1-jyu4 ngo5 zoek3 fui1-sik1 ge3 laang1-saam1 laa1?]

I don't know what clothes to wear. Why don't I wear a gray sweater?

Sample Exercises

Translate or transliterate the following sentences.

1. [ngo5 mou5 heoi3 gwo3 coeng3-kei1]

   我冇去過唱K。

   _____

2. I like coffee more.

   _____

3. I like reading more than shopping.

   _____

Chapter 10

I feel a little sick

我有少少唔舒服

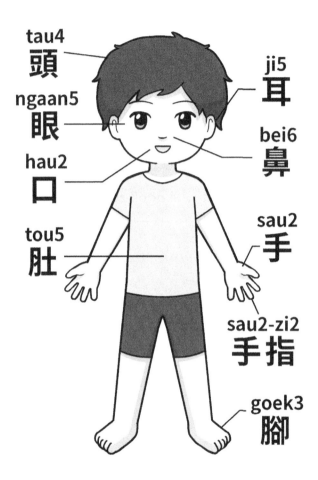

tau4
頭

ngaan5
眼

hau2
口

tou5
肚

ji5
耳

bei6
鼻

sau2
手

sau2-zi2
手指

goek3
腳

Due to the harmful effects of global warming, some starving wild animals have had to wander into human settlements to find food. Wild animals are facing miserable circumstances, not only losing their habitats but also getting sick more easily. This applies to Ben as well as he adapts to the weather and temperature of Hong Kong. In this chapter, Ben has to explain his symptoms to the doctor after getting sick. After reading this chapter, you will be able to distinguish body parts and express your level of discomfort and illness in Cantonese.

Vocabulary A 🔊

Body Part	English	Classifier	
		for one	**for a pair**
頭 [tau4]	head	個 [go3]	-
眼 [ngaan5]	eye	隻 [zek3]	對 [deoi3]
耳 [ji5]	ear	隻 [zek3]	對 [deoi3]
口 [hau2]	mouth	個 [go3]	-
鼻 [bei6]	nose	個 [go3]	-
手 [sau2]	hand	隻 [zek3]	對 [deoi3]
腳 [goek3]	foot	隻 [zek3]	對 [deoi3]
肚 [tou5]	stomach	個 [go3]	-
手指 [sau2-zi2]	finger	隻 [zek3]	-

Remember what 對 (deoi3) means from the previous chapter? Yes, it means "a pair!"

Hint: if you are struggling to remember which body part corresponds with classifiers 個 (go3) or 隻 (zek3), just remember, the ones that can form a pair use 隻 (zek3), and the ones that cannot form a pair use 個 (go3) in singular form.

Sample Sentences A 🔊

呢隻係我嘅左手。[ni1-zek3 hai6 ngo5 ge3 zo2-sau2]

This is my left hand.　　　| 左 [zo2] = left

呢隻係我嘅右腳。

[ni1-zek3 hai6 ngo5 ge3 jau6 goek3]

This is my right foot.

| 右 [jau6] = right

你對眼好大。

[nei5 deoi3 ngaan5 hou2 daai6]

Your eyes are very big.

Question: Why do you use 你對眼 (nei5 deoi3 ngaan5) here instead of 你嘅眼 (nei5 ge3 ngaan5) to refer to "your eyes?"

Answer: When it is referring to a specific noun (person/object) in its possessive form, you replace the 嘅 (ge3) with the specific classifier to the noun. In this example, using the classifier gives more details to the audience whether you are referring to one eye or both eyes.

你對手好污糟。[nei5 deoi3 sau2 hou2 wu1-zou1]

Your hands are very dirty.

你對腳可以放喺呢度。

[nei5 deoi3 goek3 ho2-ji5 fong3 hai2 ni1-dou6]

You can place your feet here.

我有10隻手指。

[ngo5 jau5 sap6-zek3 sau2-zi2]

I have ten fingers.

十隻手指有長短。

[sap6-zek3 sau2-zi2 jau5 coeng4 dyun2]

Everyone is different and has his/her strengths and weaknesses. (*idiom*)*

| 長 [coeng4] = long | 短 [dyun2] = short

Vocabulary B 🔊

頭痛 [tau4 tung3] = headache

肚痛 [tou5 tung3] = stomach ache

喉嚨痛 [hau4-lung4 tung3] = to have a sore throat

感冒 [gam2-mou6] = to catch a cold

咳 [kat1] = to cough

發燒 [faat3-siu1] = to have a fever

舒服 [syu1-fuk6] = to be comfortable

唔舒服 [m4 syu1-fuk6] = to be uncomfortable; to be sick; to be under the weather

Sample Sentences B 🔊

我今日頭痛。[ngo5 gam1-jat6 tau4 tung3]

I have a headache today.

我今日好頭痛。[ngo5 gam1-jat6 hou2 tau4 tung3]

I have a very bad headache today.**

我有少少肚痛。[ngo5 jau5 siu2-siu2 tou5 tung3]

I have a small stomach ache.

*Literal meaning: There are different lengths in ten fingers.
**Literal meaning: Today my head hurts a lot.

你感冒呀？[nei5 gam2-mou6 aa4?]

Did you catch a cold?

你邊度唔舒服呀？

[nei5 bin1-dou6 m4 syu1-fuk6 aa3?]

Where do you feel unwell?

我今日有少少唔舒服，我想請假。
[ngo5 gam1-jat6 jau5 siu2-siu2 m4 syu1-fuk6, ngo5 soeng2 ceng2-gaa3]

I feel a little sick today, I want to ask for leave.

| 請假 [ceng2-gaa3] = to ask for leave

我而家發燒，想請病假。

[ngo5 ji4-gaa1 faat3-siu1, soeng2-ceng2-beng6 gaa3]

I am having a fever now, (and) I want to ask for sick leave.

Vocabulary C 🔊

全部 [cyun4-bou6] = all

有啲 [jau5-di1] = some

冇 [mou5] = none

好 [hou2] = very

幾 [gei2] = quite

有少少 [jau5 siu2-siu2] = a little

唔 [m4] = not

Sample Sentences C 🔊

我有少少發燒。

[ngo5 jau5 siu2-siu2 faat3-siu1]

I have a slight fever.

我有少少唔舒服。

[ngo5 jau5 siu2-siu2 m4 syu1-fuk6]

I feel a little sick.

呢度幾好。

[ni1-dou6 gei2 hou2]

It's quite nice here.

喺呢度返工幾好。

[hai2 ni1-dou6 faan1-gung1 gei2 hou2]

It's quite nice working here.

學校全部人都唔舒服。

[hok6-haau6 cyun4-bou6 jan4 dou1 m4 syu1-fuk6]

Everyone in school is sick.

Remember in a previous chapter we learned to use 都 (dou1) before the verb to emphasize "every … without exception?" Here it is used to imply, "Everyone at school is sick, without exception," to emphasize the severity of the situation when everyone has gotten sick.

However, there are many usages of 都 (dou1)

     / without exception (adv.)

都 [dou1] – both; also (adv.)

     \ even (adv.)

both; also (adv.)

我都感冒。[ngo5 dou1 gam2-mou6]

I also have a cold.

even (adv.)

我好少感冒，今年我都感冒。

[ngo5 hou2-siu2 gam2-mou6, gam1-nin2 ngo5 dou1 gam2-mou6]

I rarely catch a cold; (but) this year even I caught a cold.

Recognizing and Writing Chinese Characters

Spoken	Written	Definition	Stroke Order	Word Pair
-	口 [hau2]	mouth	丨 冂 口	
-	手 [sau2]	hand	丿 ⸗ 三 手	
唔 [m4]	不 [bat1]	not	一 丆 不 不	
-	耳 [ji5]	ear	一 丆 丌 丌 耳 耳	
-	肚 [tou5]	stomach	丿 冂 月 月 肚 肚 肚	
-	都 [dou1]	also; both	一 十 土 尹 者 者 者 者 都	
-	隻 [zek3]	classifier for animals and one of a pair	丿 亻 亻 仁 仨 住 隹 隻 隻	一隻 [jat1-zek3] one (animal)

Writing Practice

Sample Conversation 🔊

Dr. Chan:

你好，Ben。你邊度唔舒服呀？

[nei5 hou2, Ben. nei5 bin1-dou6 m4 syu1-fuk6 aa3?]

Hi, Ben. Where are you feeling unwell?

Ben:

陳醫生，你好。我有少少肚痛。

[can4 ji1-sang1, nei5 hou2. ngo5 jau5 siu2-siu2 tou5 tung3]

Hi, Dr. Chan. I have a slight stomach ache.

Dr. Chan:

幾時開始痛呀？[gei2-si4 hoi1-ci2 tung3 aa3?]

When did the pain start?

| 開始 [hoi1-ci2] = to start

Ben:

今日朝早開始。

[gam1-jat6 ziu1-zou2 hoi1-ci2]

It started this morning.

Dr. Chan:

你早餐食咗咩呀？

[nei5 zou2-caan1 sik6 zo2 me1 aa3?]

What did you eat for breakfast?

Ben:

食咗雞蛋。

[sik6 zo2 gai1 daan2]

(I) ate some eggs.

Cultural Insights | What is *yit-hei* and what do you do when you are *yit-hei*?

Traditional Chinese Medicine, or TCM 中醫 (zung1-ji1), includes both herbs and health and wellness practices such as Qi Gong and acupuncture. There are over 300 herbs that are common in Chinese medicinal practice. The effectiveness of traditional Chinese medicine for treating different diseases is debatable, but the goal of using TCM is to regain balance in your body. An extremely common diagnosis in TCM is 熱氣 (jit6-hei3), or sometimes romanized as yit-hei or yeet-hay. A very common symptom of 熱氣 (jit6-hei3) is sore throat.

In TCM, 熱氣 (jit6-hei3), which literally means "hot air" in Chinese, refers to the yin-yang imbalance of a person caused by the hot properties of food. There are some foods, such as those that have hot properties, that trigger this imbalance because excess heat in the system damages the liver. Hot food includes red and black peppers, alcohol, and any deep-fried food, which are spicy, hot, and warming. On the other hand, cool food includes peppermint, which makes you feel cooled and refreshed.

Some common remedies to treat 熱氣 (jit6-hei3) are herbal tea and soup. You can easily find herbal tea shops anywhere in Guangdong and Hong Kong. If you live overseas, you can also find them in most Chinese bakeries and in packaged form in Chinese supermarkets.

See answers on page #210

Chapter 10 Exercises

1. What is the classifier for the head, mouth, nose, and stomach in the singular form?

   _____

2. What is the classifier for the eye, ear, hand, and foot in the singular form?

   _____

3. What is the classifier for a pair of items?

   _____

4. How do you express "I have a headache?"

   _____

5. In what situation do you use 有 (jau5) for "having a headache?"

   _____

6. Translate or transliterate the following sentences:

   [___ ___ ___ ___ ___]

   我十點瞓覺。

   I go to bed at ten o'clock.

   [nei5 gei2 dim2 hei2-san1 aa3?]

   你幾點起身呀？

   _____

[ngo5 ji4-gaa1 caat3 gan2 ngaa4]

我而家刷緊牙。

___

[___ ___ ___ ___ ___?]

佢做緊咩呀？

What is he/she doing?

[ngo5 tou5 tung3 m4 faan1-gung1]

我肚痛唔返工。

___

Chapter 11

The weather today is very...

今日天氣好...

Located in southern China, Hong Kong is very humid. The arrival of autumn marks the end of the rainy season, and November is considered the best time to visit Hong Kong. In this chapter, I will teach you ways to describe the weather and seasons, as well as the names of popular sports. After reading this chapter, you should be able to tell others your favorite season and sports in Cantonese, along with the current weather.

To start off, let's review how we describe someone's state from Chapter 4.

我 [ngo5] = I; me

好 [hou2] = very; good

我 [ngo5] + 好 [hou2] + state of being = I am very...

Applying the same rule we use to say "I am very ... today," we form the phrase "今日好 (gam1–jat6 hou2)... Today is very ..." in Cantonese.

Remember how to say "hot" and "cold?" Don't worry if you don't, we will keep refreshing your memory from Book 1.

凍 [dung3] = cold

熱 [jit6] = hot

Now let's use this structure to describe how the weather feels.

今日 [gam1-jat6] + 好 [hou2] + 凍 [dung3] = It's very cold today.

今日 [gam1-jat6] + 好 [hou2] + 熱 [jit6] = It's very hot today.

Now, let's learn more adjectives to describe the weather and why Hong Kong is a great place to conduct research on global warming.

Vocabulary A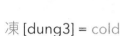

凍 [dung3] = cold

熱 [jit6] = hot

暖 [nyun5] = warm

天氣 [tin1-hei3] = weather

涼爽 [loeng4-song2] = cool

落雨 [lok6-jyu5] = to rain

落雪 [lok6-syut3] = to snow

全球暖化 [cyun4-kau4 nyun5-faa3] = global warming

Sample Sentences A 🔊

今日嘅天氣點呀？

[gam1-jat6 ge3 tin1-hei3 dim2 aa3?] | 天氣 [tin1-hei3] = weather

How is today's weather?

香港嘅天氣點呀？

[hoeng1-gong2 ge3 tin1-hei3 dim2 aa3?]

How is Hong Kong's weather?

香港嘅天氣好暖。

[hoeng1-gong2 ge3 tin1-hei3 hou2 nyun5]

The weather in Hong Kong is very warm.

呢度嘅天氣好好。

[ni1-dou6 ge3 tin1-hei3 hou2 hou2]

The weather here is very nice.

香港唔落雪。

[hoeng1-gong2 m4 lok6-syut3]

It doesn't snow in Hong Kong.

香港成日落雨。

[hoeng1-gong2 seng4-jat6 lok6-jyu5]

It always rains in Hong Kong.

雖然香港天氣好暖，但係經常落雨。

[seoi1-jin4 hoeng1-gong2 tin1-hei3 hou2 nyun5, daan6-hai6 ging1-soeng4 lok6-jyu5]

Although the weather in Hong Kong is very warm, it often rains.

琴晚好涼爽。[kam4-maan5 hou2 loeng4-song2]

It was very cool last night.

今朝有少少暖。[gam1-ziu1 jau5 siu2-siu2 nyun5]

It was a little warm this morning.

我好擔心全球暖化。

[ngo5 hou2 daam1-sam1 cyun4-kau4 nyun5-faa3]

I am very worried about global warming.

| 擔心 [daam1-sam1] = to worry

Now that we have learned about the weather, let's learn the names of some popular sports in Hong Kong.

Vocabulary B 🔊

球/波 [kau4/bo1] = ball

足球 [zuk1-kau4] = soccer
踢足球 [tek3 zuk1-kau4] = to play soccer

排球 [paai4-kau4] = volleyball
打排球 [daa2 paai4-kau4] = to play volleyball

籃球 [laam4- kau4] = basketball
打籃球 [daa2 laam4-kau4] = to play basketball

乒乓球 [bing1-bam1 kau4] = ping-pong
打乒乓球 [daa2 bing1-bam1 kau4] = to play ping-pong

網球 [mong5-kau4] = tennis
打網球 [daa2 mong5-kau4] = to play tennis

羽毛球 [jyu5-mou4 kau4] = badminton
打羽毛球 [daa2 jyu5-mou4 kau4] = to play badminton

| 羽毛 [jyu5-mou4] = feather

高爾夫球 [gou1-ji5-fu1 kau4] = golf
打高爾夫球 [daa2 gou1-ji5-fu1 kau4] = to play golf

Sample Sentences B 🔊

你鍾唔鍾意打乒乓球呀？

[nei5 zung1-m4-zung1-ji3 daa2 bing1-bam1 kau4 aa3?]

Do you like to play ping-pong?

我唔識打羽毛球。

[ngo5 m4 sik1 daa2 jyu5-mou4 kau4]

I don't know how to play badminton.

今日天氣好涼爽，不如去打籃球啦？

[gam1-jat6 tin1-hei3 hou2 loeng4-song2, bat1-jyu4 heoi3 daa2 laam4-kau4 laa1?]

The weather today is so cool. Why don't we go and play basketball?

琴日落雨，我冇去踢足球。

[kam4-jat6 lok6-jyu5, ngo5 mou5 heoi3 tek3 zuk1-kau4]

It rained yesterday, (so) I didn't go play soccer.

喺香港邊度可以打網球呀？

[hai2 hoeng1-gong2 bin1-dou6 ho2-ji5 daa2 mong5-kau4 aa3?]

Where can you play tennis in Hong Kong?

我嘅朋友都鍾意打排球。

[ngo5 ge3 pang4-jau5 dou1 zung1-ji3 daa2 paai4-kau4]

All of my friends like to play volleyball.

邊個識打高爾夫球呀？

[bin1-go3 sik1 daa2 gou1-ji5-fu1 kau4 aa3?]

Who knows how to play golf?

Now that you have learned about the weather and some popular sports, let's also incorporate the seasons of the year.

Vocabulary C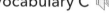

季節 [gwai3-zit3] = season

春天 [ceon1-tin1] = spring

夏天 [haa6-tin1] = summer

秋天 [cau1-tin1] = autumn

冬天 [dung1-tin1] = winter

假 [gaa3] = vacation

春假 [ceon1-gaa3] = spring break

暑假 [syu2-gaa3] = summer vacation

寒假 [hon4-gaa3] = winter break

> The two biggest vacations in China are 暑假 (syu2-gaa3) summer vacation and 寒假 (hon4-gaa3) winter break. So 春假 (ceon1-gaa3) Spring break is not common in China since the Chinese/Lunar New Year usually falls during the winter break instead.

Sample Sentences C 🔊

你鍾意邊個季節呀？

[nei5 zung1-ji3 bin1-go3 gwai3-zit3 aa3?]

Which season do you like?

你最鍾意邊個季節呀？

[nei5 zeoi3 zung1-ji3 bin1-go3 gwai3-zit3 aa3?]

Which season do you like the most?

呢個暑假我要學游水。

[ni1-go3 syu2-gaa3 ngo5 jiu3 hok6 jau4-seoi2]

This summer, I have to learn how to swim.

香港一年有四個季節。

[hoeng1-gong2 jat1 nin4 jau5 sei3-go3 gwai3-zit3]

A year in Hong Kong has four (distinct) seasons.

春天經常落雨。

[ceon1-tin1 ging1-soeng4 lok6-jyu5]

It often rains in spring.

寒假你想去邊度呀？

[hon4-gaa3 nei5 soeng2 heoi3 bin1-dou6 aa3?]

Where do you want to go for winter break?

春假最好係打網球。

[ceon1-gaa3 zeoi3 hou2 hai6 daa2 mong5-kau4]

It is best to play tennis on spring break.

今日好涼爽，不如我哋去打籃球啦！

[gam1-jat6 hou2 loeng4-song2, bat1-jyu4 ngo5-dei6 heoi3 daa2 laam4-kau4 laa1!]

It is so cool today, why don't we go and play basketball?

Recognizing and Writing Chinese Characters

Spoken	Written	Definition	Stroke Order	Word Pair
-	天 [tin1]	sky	一 二 チ 天	冬天 [dung1-tin1] winter
-	冬 [dung1]	winter	丿 ク 夂 冬 冬	
-	雨 [jyu5]	rain	一 厂 币 币 雨 雨 雨 雨	
-	春 [ceon1]	spring	一 二 三 丰 夫 表 春 春 春	春天 [ceon1-tin1] spring
-	秋 [cau1]	autumn	丿 一 千 千 禾 禾 秒 秋 秋	秋天 [cau1-tin1] autumn
-	夏 [haa6]	summer	一 一 丆 丏 百 百 百 頁 夏 夏	夏天 [haa6-tin1] summer
-	氣 [hei3]	gas	丿 一 气 气 氕 氣 氣 氣 氣	天氣 [tin1-hei3] weather

Writing Practice

Sample Conversation 🔊

Stormy:

聽日星期六，我哋去邊度玩呀？

[ting1-jat6 sing1-kei4-luk6, ngo5-dei6 heoi3 bin1-dou6 waan2 aa3?]

It's Saturday tomorrow. Where should we go to hang out?

Ben:

聽日天氣點呀？[ting1-jat6 tin1-hei3 dim2 aa3?]

How's the weather tomorrow?

Stormy:

我睇下。聽日天氣好好，好涼爽。

[ngo5 tai2 haa5. ting1-jat6 tin1-hei3 hou2 hou2, hou2 loeng4-song2]

Let me take a look. The weather tomorrow is very nice, (and) it's very cool.

Ben:

不如我哋去打籃球啦！

[bat1-jyu4 ngo5-dei6 heoi3 daa2 laam4-kau4 laa1!]

Why don't we go play basketball?

Stormy:

好呀，秋天我最鍾意打籃球。

[hou2 aa3, cau1-tin1 ngo5 zeoi3 zung1-ji3 daa2 laam4-kau4]

Great, in the fall I like to play basketball the most.

Cultural Insights | Umbrella: From the weather to political movements

Whether you are visiting China for the first time or living in a Chinese community, you may wonder why Chinese people (stereotypically ladies) carry umbrellas on both rainy and sunny days. Using umbrellas in the sun is very common in many Asian countries, especially in tropical and subtropical areas.

Using an umbrella in the sun can help you to stay cool and avoid getting sunburnt. Unlike western cultures where tanned skin can symbolize a healthy, desirable lifestyle, east Asian culture has a different perspective. Light-toned skin is considered more desirable in many east Asian cultures because it stands for flawlessness and purity. Therefore, you can find very delicate and well-designed umbrellas in China to help block sunlight, which may cause freckles on skin. Many of them are even designed to be UV-proof.

Umbrellas are not only utilitarian, but have also served as political symbols. In 2014, there arose a major political movement in Hong Kong. It was called "The Umbrella Movement" and involved a series of sit-in street protests. Umbrellas were used to protect protesters against pepper spray used by the police. They were also color-coded to represent one's political opinion in a political movement—carrying a yellow umbrella indicated your support of the Democratic party, and blue your support of the Beijing government.

See answers on page #211

Chapter 11 Exercises

1. Do you need a copular verb (am/is/are) to state how the weather is today? (i.e., it's very hot today.)

    _____

2. How do you ask someone, "How is today's weather?"

    _____

3. What are the four seasons in Cantonese?

    _____

4. What is the verb for "playing basketball?"

    _____

5. What is the verb for "playing soccer?"

    _____

6. Draw a line to connect the appropriate Chinese character to its translation:

春	sky
雨	fall
雪	summer
天	rain
秋	winter
冬	snow
夏	spring

7. Translate or transliterate the following sentences:

[gam1 jat6 ge3 tin1 hei3 hou2 hou2]

今日嘅天氣好好。

_____

[___ ___ ___ ___ ___ ___]

我最鍾意夏天。

I like summer the most.

[hoeng1 gong2 ge3 dung1 tin1 m4 lok6 syut3]

_____

Chapter 12

When ..., you can ...

...嗰陣，你可以...

As December, the final season of the semester, approaches, my students are preparing to present their final project on environmental sustainability.

My student Wai, a green sea turtle, had scheduled an appointment during my office hours to discuss everyday practices that are useful for saving the environment.

After reading my conversation with Wai in this chapter, you will be able to use Cantonese to speak with others about ways they can save the environment in their everyday lives. You will also learn how to save the many endangered and vulnerable animals on the planet, including polar bears.

Before we start, let's learn a commonly used command structure and incorporate a few verbs to tell others about energy usage.

唔好... [m4-hou2] = don't ...

Vocabulary A 🔊

用 [jung6] = to use

慳 [haan1] = to save (by not using); frugal

嘥 [saai1] = to waste; wasteful

開 [hoi1] = to open; to turn on

關 [gwaan1] = to close; to turn off

> 慳 (haan1) means to save. In English, "saving" can imply two different methods: by not spending, or by setting some money aside. For example, you can either "save" money by using coupons to spend less, or you can "save" money by depositing it in the bank. 慳 (haan1) takes on the meaning of the former, that is saving money by not spending.

Sample Sentences A 🔊

我平時好慳。[ngo5 ping4-si4 hou2 haan1]

I am normally very frugal.

你用唔用呢個app呀？

[nei5 jung6-m4-jung6 ni1-go3 app aa3?]

Do you use this app?

我唔鍾意嘥嘢。[ngo5 m4 zung1-ji3 saai1 je5]

I don't like to waste things.

唔好嘥嘢啦！[m4-hou2 saai1 je5 laa1!]

Don't waste things!

我要慳錢買屋。[ngo5 jiu3 haan1 cin2 maai5 uk1]

I have to save money to buy a house.

如果你想慳錢，你可以買少啲衫。

[jyu4-gwo2 nei5 soeng2 haan1 cin2, nei5 ho2-ji5 maai5 siu2-di1 saam1]

If you want to save some money, you can buy less clothes.

我哋11點開門。

[ngo5-dei6 sap6-jat1 dim2 hoi1-mun4]

We open at 11 o'clock.

| 門 [mun4] = door

你哋幾點關門呀？

[nei5-dei6 gei2 dim2 gwaan1-mun4 aa3?]

What time do you close?

Now, let's learn the names of natural resources and alternatives that we can use to lessen our impact on the environment.

Vocabulary B 🔊

電 [din6] = electricity

水 [seoi2] = water

火 [fo2] = fire

煤氣 [mui4-hei3] = coal gas

天然氣 [tin1-jin4 hei3] = natural gas

石油 [sek6-jau4] = petroleum

一次性 [jat1-ci3-sing3] = disposable*

膠 [gaau1] = plastic

袋 [doi2] = bag

膠袋 [gaau1 doi2] = plastic bag

環保袋 [waan4-bou2 doi2] = reusable bag

Remember in Chapter 7 where we learned that 環保 (waan4-bou2) means "eco-friendly?" The concept of eco-friendliness is built into reusable products, and thus a reusable bag is called 環保袋 (waan4-bou2 doi2), literally an eco-friendly bag.

Sample Sentences B 🔊

我哋可以多啲用環保袋。

[ngo5-dei6 ho2-ji5 do1-di1 jung6 waan4-bou2 doi2]

We can use reusable bags more.

Do you remember from Chapter 8 we place "多啲 (do1-di1) more" at the end of the sentence? In this section, we try to place it before the verb and say "to do ... more."

我哋可以用少啲電。

[ngo5-dei6 ho2-ji5 jung6 siu2-di1 din6]

We can use less electricity.

* Literal Meaning: Single Use

唔好用一次性膠袋啦！

[m4-hou2 jung6 jat1-ci3-sing3 gaau1 doi2 laa1!]

Don't use disposable plastic bags!

坐地鐵同巴士可以慳石油。

[co5 dei6-tit3 tung4 baa1-si2 ho2-ji5 haan1 sek6-jau4]

Taking the subway and bus can save petroleum.

我阿媽用天然氣煲湯。

[ngo5 aa3-maa1 jung6 tin1-jin4 hei3 bou1 tong1]

My mom uses natural gas to cook soup.

| 煲 [bou1] = to boil

我哋屋企好慳電。

[ngo5-dei6 uk1-kei2 hou2 haan1 din6]

Our household is very energy-efficient*.

慳水有好多方法。

[haan1 seoi2 jau5 hou2 do1 fong1-faat3]

There are many ways to save water.

| 方法 [fong1-faat3] = method

Because energy saving can vary across different cultures, the following section covers easily accessible methods for both Eastern and Western cultures to better treat our planet.

Let's go ahead and learn about some alternatives to make our daily lifestyle more eco-friendly, or 環保 (waan4-bou2), as you would say in Cantonese.

* Literal meaning: Our household saves a lot of electricity.

Vocabulary C 🔊

慳電膽 [haan1 din6 daam2] = energy-saving light bulb

曬衫 [saai3 saam1] = to sun-dry clothes

竹蓆 [zuk1 zek6] = bamboo mat

花灑 [faa1-saa2] = shower head (loan word from "faucet")

餐具 [caan1-geoi6] = utensil

吸管 [kap1-gun2] = straw

壓力煲 [aat3-lik6 bou1] = pressure cooker

Now, let's learn a new sentence structure to apply our new vocabulary.

Using a bamboo mat, or 竹蓆 (zuk1 zek6), is a very common alternative to reduce heat during sleep in the summer. A bamboo mat is illustrated on the left side of the image above.

…嗰陣，你可以… [… go2-zan6, nei5 ho2-ji5 …] = When …, you can …

買嘢 [maai5 je5] + 嗰陣 [go2-zan6]，你可以 [nei5 ho2-ji5] + 用環保袋 [jung6 waan4-bou2 doi2] = When shopping, you can use a reusable bag.

Sample Sentences C 🔊

去返工嗰陣，我哋可以坐地鐵。

[heoi3 faan1-gung1 go2-zan6, ngo5-dei6 ho2-ji5 co5 dei6-tit3]

When going to work, we can ride the subway.

喺屋企嗰陣，我哋可以用慳電膽。

[hai2 uk1-kei2 go2-zan6, ngo5-dei6 ho2-ji5 jung6 haan1 din6 daam2]

When at home, we can use energy-saving light bulbs.

瞓覺嗰陣，我哋可以關燈。

[fan3-gaau3 go2-zan6, ngo5-dei6 ho2-ji5 gwaan1 dang1]

When sleeping, we can turn off the light.

夏天嗰陣，我哋可以曬衫。

[haa6-tin1 go2-zan6, ngo5-dei6 ho2-ji5 saai3 saam1]

When it is summer, we can sun-dry clothes.

熱嗰陣，我哋可以用竹蓆瞓覺。

[jit6 go2-zan6, ngo5-dei6 ho2-ji5 jung6 zuk1 zek6 fan3-gaau3]

When it is hot, we can use a bamboo mat for sleeping.

用洗頭水嗰陣，我哋可以關花灑。

[jung6 sai2-tau4 seoi2 go2-zan6, ngo5-dei6 ho2-ji5 gwaan1 faa1-saa2]

When shampooing, we can turn off the shower head.

| 洗頭水 [sai2-tau4 seoi2] = shampoo

食外賣嗰陣，可以用環保餐具。

[sik6 ngoi6-maai6 go2-zan6, ho2-ji5 jung6 waan4-bou2 caan1-geoi6]

When eating takeout, (we) can use recyclable utensils.

| 外賣 [ngoi6-maai6] = takeout

飲凍咖啡嗰陣，我用環保吸管。

[jam2 dung3 gaa3-fe1 go2-zan6, ngo5 jung6 waan4-bou2 kap1-gun2]

When drinking iced coffee, I use a reusable straw.

煲湯嗰陣，我哋可以用壓力煲。

[bou1 tong1 go2-zan6, ngo5-dei6 ho2-ji5 jung6 aat3-lik6 bou1]

When making soup, we can use a pressure cooker.

Recognizing and Writing Chinese Characters

Spoken	Written	Definition	Stroke Order								Word Pair
-	火 [fo2]	fire	丶	丷	丿	火					
-	用 [jung6]	to use	丿	刀	月	月	用				
-	石 [sek6]	stone	一	丆	石	石	石				石油 [sek6-jau4] petroleum
-	油 [jau4]	oil	丶	丶	氵	氵	汩	油	油	油	
-	門 [mun4]	door	丨	冂	冃	冃	門	門	門		
-	洗 [sai2]	to wash	丶	丶	氵	氵	汻	汢	洪	洗	
-	保 [bou2]	to protect	丿	亻	亻	伫	伫	伫	仔	保	環保 [waan4-bou2] eco-friendly

Writing Practice

Sample Conversation 🔊

Wai:

Ben Sir, 你好。[Ben Sir, nei5-hou2]

Hi, Mr. Ben.

Ben:

阿偉，今日你想學咩呀？

[aa3-wai5, gam1-jat6 nei5 soeng2 hok6 me1 aa3?]

Wai, what would you like to learn today?

Wai:

我想傾下環保嘅方法。

[ngo5 soeng2 king1 haa5 waan4-bou2 ge3 fong1-faat3]

I want to talk about some ways to be eco-friendly.

│ 傾 [king1] = to chat

Ben:

你覺得我哋點樣可以環保啲呀？

[nei5 gok3-dak1 ngo5-dei6 dim2-joeng2 ho2-ji5 waan4-bou2 di1 aa3?]

How do you think we can be more eco-friendly?

Wai:

我哋行街可以用環保袋，唔用膠袋。

[ngo5-dei6 haang4-gaai1 ho2-ji5 jung6 waan4-bou2 doi2, m4 jung6 gaau1 doi2]

When shopping, we can use reusable bags and not use plastic bags.

Ben:

仲有呢？[zung6-jau5 ne1?]

What else?

Wai:

飲咖啡同珍珠奶茶嗰陣，我哋可以用環保吸管。

[jam2 gaa3-fe1 tung4 zan1-zyu1 naai5-caa4 go2-zan6, ngo5-dei6 ho2-ji5 jung6 waan4-bou2 kap1-gun2]

When drinking coffee and bubble tea, we can use reusable straws.

Ben:

好提議！[ngo5 tai4-ji5!]

Good idea!

Wai:

Ben Sir，點解你嚟香港呀？

[Ben Sir, dim2-gaai2 nei5 lei4 hoeng1-gong2 aa3?]

Mr. Ben, why have you come to Hong Kong?

Ben:

因為我想喺香港宣傳環保。

[jan1-wai6 ngo5 soeng2 hai2 hoeng1-gong2 syun1-cyun4 waan4-bou2]

Because I want to promote eco-friendliness in Hong Kong.

| 宣傳 [syun1-cyun4] = to promote

Wai:

你覺得香港點樣呀？

[nei5 gok3-dak1 hoeng1-gong2 dim2-joeng2 aa3?]

What do you think of Hong Kong?

Ben:

我好鍾意香港，因為香港人好勤力，香港嘅嘢好好味。

[ngo5 hou2 zung1-ji3 hoeng1-gong2, jan1-wai6 hoeng1-gong2 jan4 hou2 kan4-lik6, hoeng1-gong2 ge3 je5 hou2 hou2-mei6]

I really like Hong Kong, because people in Hong Kong are very hard-working and food in Hong Kong is very delicious.

你呢，阿偉？點解你嚟香港？

[nei5 ne1, aa3-wai5? dim2-gaai2 nei5 lei4 hoeng1-gong2?]

What about you, Wai? Why have you come to Hong Kong?

Wai:

我嚟香港學點樣可以環保。

[ngo5 lei4 hoeng1-gong2 hok6 dim2-joeng2 ho2-ji5 waan4-bou2]

I came to Hong Kong to learn how to be eco-friendly.

如果全球繼續暖化，你同我都會絕種。

[jyu4-gwo2 cyun4-kau4 gai3-zuk6 nyun5-faa3, nei5 tung4 ngo5 dou1 wui5 zyut6-zung2]

If global warming continues, you and I will both be extinct.

| 繼續 [gai3-zuk6] = to continue

| 絕種 [zyut6-zung2] = extinct

好快冇人知咩係北極熊同青海龜。

[hou2 faai3 mou5 jan4 zi1 me1 hai6 bak1-gik6 hung4 tung4 cing1-hoi2 gwai1]

Very soon, no one will know what polar bears and green sea turtles are.

Cultural Insights | Addressing school teachers with "阿Sir (aa3-sir)" and "Miss (mit1-si4)" in Hong Kong

In English, we mention a person's last name after his or her title, for example, Mr. Chan and Ms. Lee. However, in Chinese, we always mention last names first. For example, 陳生 (can4 saang1) for Mr. Chan, which literally translates as "Chan Mister," and 陳小姐 (can4 siu2-ze2) for Miss Chan, which literally translates as "Chan Miss."

The word for teacher is 老師 (lou5-si1) in Chinese. Traditionally, a way to address a teacher with respect is to say 老師 (lou5-si1) after the teacher's last name. For example, if the teacher's last name is Lee, he or she will be called 李老師 (lei5 lou5-si1), regardless of the person's gender. However, teachers are usually addressed with different titles in Hong Kong. For example, a female teacher would be addressed in English as "Ms. Lee," and a male teacher would be called 李Sir (lei5 sir).

See answers on page #212

Chapter 12 Exercises

1. What is the verb for "closing doors" in Cantonese?

   _____

2. What does 慳 (haan1) mean?

   _____

3. What does 環保 (waan4-bou2) mean?

   _____

4. What does 嗰陣 (go2-zan6) mean? Is it used in a statement or question?

   _____

5. Translate or transliterate the following sentences:

   [ngo5 hou2 haan1]
   我好慳。

   _____

   [dim2-joeng2 ho2-ji5 haan1 cin2 aa3?]
   點樣可以慳錢呀?

   _____

   [___ ___ ___ ___ ___ ___ ___ ___ ___?]
   你屋企有冇慳電膽呀?
   Do you have energy-saving light bulbs at home?

[___ ___ ___ ___ ___ ___]

我有環保吸管。

I have (a) reusable straw.

Part IV Review: Winter

- The classifier for head, mouth, nose, and stomach is 個 (go3).

- The classifier for one eye, ear, hand, foot, and finger is 隻 (zek3).

- The classifier for one pair of eyes, ears, hands, and feet is 對 (deoi3).

- To express discomfort that is caused by pain, you can say noun + 痛 (tung3).

- To ask for leave, you can use the verb "請假 (ceng2-gaa3)."

- To express "a little" in amount and severity, you can say 有少少 (jau5 siu2-siu2)

- 都 (dou1) means "both," "also," or emphasizes "all without exception."

- to know (a skill or knowledge) = 識 (sik1)

- 打 (daa2) is the verb that is used to indicate "to play" a sport.

- 慳 (haan1) can be used as either an adjective or a verb, "frugal" or "to save."

- to use = 用 (jung6)

- For anything that is disposable, you can use "一次性 (jat1-ci3-sing3)."

- To use "when" in a statement to point out a time period, you can say "...嗰陣 (... go2-zan6)."

- To address your teacher, you can say his or her last name first, and then add "老師 (lou5-si1)."

See answers on page #212

Sample Paragraph

陳老師，我今日唔舒服。我有少少頭痛同發燒。我想請假。

[can4 lou5-si1, ngo5 gam1-jat6 m4 syu1-fuk6. ngo5 jau5 siu2-siu2 tau4 tung3 tung4 faat3-siu1. ngo5 soeng2 ceng2-gaa3]

Ms./Mr. Chan (teacher), I am not feeling well today. I have a slight headache and fever. I want to ask for leave.

我識打排球、籃球、同網球。夏天嗰陣，我鍾意打排球。

[ngo5 sik1 daa2 paai4-kau4, laam4-kau4, tung4 mong5-kau4. haa6-tin1 go2-zan6, ngo5 zung1-ji3 daa2 paai4-kau4]

I know how to play volleyball, basketball, and tennis. When it is summer, I like to play volleyball.

Sample Exercise

1. I have a stomach ache.

    _____

2. 你對眼好大。

    [neoi5 deoi3 ngaan5 hou2 daai6]

    _____

3. 冬天嗰陣，我鍾意飲熱奶茶。

    [dung1-tin1 go2-zan6, ngo5 zung1-ji3 jam2 jit6 naai5-caa4]

    _____

List of Interrogative Words

咩 [me1] = what

邊度 [bin1-dou6] = where

點樣 [dim2-joeng2] = how

幾時 [gei2-si4] = when

點解 [dim2-gaai2] = why

邊個 [bin1-go3] = who; which

幾點 [gei2-dim2] = what time

Answer Key

Chapter 1

1.   Final particle

2.   Can I …?

3.   hai2 (喺)

4.   hou4 (毫)

5.   I am to your right.

        Your luggage is to your right.

        nei5 ho2 ji5 fong3 hai2 ni1 dou6

6.   luk6 man1

        sap6-saam1 man1 gau2 hou4

        baat3-sap6-cat1 man1 ji6 hou4 sei3

        sap6-jat1 man1 ng5 hou4 cat1

Chapter 2

1.   12

2.   nei5 suk6 me1? (你屬咩?)

3.   ge3 (嘅)

4.   ge3 (嘅)

5.   san1 tai2 gin6 hong1

        san1 nin4 faai3 lok6

        ngo5 jau5 jat1 zek3 gau2

        ngo5 jau5 jat1 zek3 fe1 sik1 ge3 gau2

Chapter 3

1.   zyu2-sau1 (主修)

2.   fu3-sau1 (副修)

3.   ge3 (嘅)

4.   ngo5 jau5 loeng5-go3 hok6-wai2
        (我有兩個學位。)

5.   I have a linguistics master's degree.
        ngo5 jau5 jat1 go3 ging1 zai3 hok6 sek6 si6 hok6 wai2
        ngo5 jau5 sap6 nin4 ge3 gung1 zok3 ging1 jim6

Part I Review: Spring

Sample Exercise

He/she is in front of me.

nei5 suk6 me1 aa3

I have three years of experience.

Chapter 4

1.   no

2.   a final particle

3.   question

4.   yes

5.   I am very angry.
        He/she is very busy today.
        ngo5 gam1 jat6 taai3 gui6 laa3

Chapter 5

1. ngo5 zyu6 hai2 (我住喺)

2. gaan1 (間)

3. ping4-fong1 cek3 (平方呎)

4. This is the kitchen.

   That is the bathroom.

   ngo5 zyu6 hai2 gau2 lung4

5. ng5-baak3

   ng5-baak3 saam1-sap6

   ng5-baak3 saam1-sap6-luk6

   ng5-cin1 cat1-baak3

   ng5-cin1 cat1-baak3 baat3-sap6

   ng5-cin1 cat1-baak3 baat3-sap6-gau2

Chapter 6

1. gaan1 (間)

2. gan1 (斤)

3. laa3 (喇)

4. I would like a milk tea that's less sweet.

   You bought one catty of pork?

   Two catties of beef is too much!

   ni1 bui1 gaa3 fe1 taai3 fu2

Part II Review: Summer

1.   ngo5 gok3 dak1 ni1 go3 daan1 wai2 hou2 hou2

2.   This house has 1,000 ft^2.

3.   nei5 taai3 hou2 jan4 laa3

Chapter 7

1.   number + dim2 (點)

2.   **Option 1**: sei3 dim2 saam1-sap6 fan1 (4點30分)
         Option 2: sei3 dim2 bun3 (4點半)
         Option 3: sei3 dim2 luk6-go3 zi6 (4點6個字)

3.   gei2 dim2 (幾點)

4.   Draw a line to connect the appropriate Chinese words to its translation:

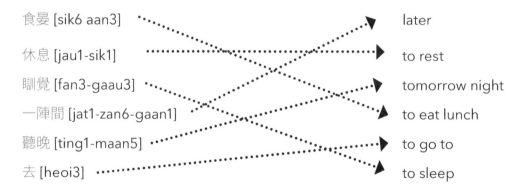

食晏 [sik6 aan3]   later

休息 [jau1-sik1]   to rest

瞓覺 [fan3-gaau3]   tomorrow night

一陣間 [jat1-zan6-gaan1]   to eat lunch

聽晚 [ting1-maan5]   to go to

去 [heoi3]   to sleep

5.   What time do you go to work?
         What time do you get up when you go to work?
         ngo5 jat1 zan6 gaan1 heoi3 nei5 uk1 kei2
         I slept at 12:30 last night.

6.   cat1 dim2 sei3-sap6-sei3 fan1
         baat3 dim2 ng5-sap6-luk6 fan1
         gau2 dim2 sap6-saam1 fan1
         loeng5 dim2 sap6 fan1 or loeng5 dim2 loeng5-go3 zi6

Chapter 8

1.	do1-gwo3 (多過)

2.	bat1-jyu4 ngo5-dei6 ... laa1? (不如我哋…啦!)

3.	mountain

4.	ngo5 mou5 ... gwo3 (我冇…過)

5.	dou1 (都)

6.	ngo5 ping4 si4 zung1 ji3 tai2 syu1

	What do you usually do on Sundays?

	ngo5 zung1 ji3 haang4 saan1 do1 gwo3 haang4 gaai1

Chapter 9

1.	taai3 (太)

2.	gin6 (件)

3.	tiu4 (條)

4.	saam1 (衫)

5.	I would like a pair of sneakers.

	Is there size 37.5?

	ngo5 soeng2 si3 zoek3 ni1 gin6 laang1 saam1

	ni1 deoi3 haai4 taai3 sai3

6.	gaa1 daai6

	sai3

	zung1

	saam1 sap6 sei3

	baat3 hou6 bun3

Part III Review: Autumn

Sample Exercise

1.   I have never gone to karaoke.

2.   ngo5 zung1-ji3 gaa3-fe1 do1-di1

(我鍾意咖啡多啲。)

3.   ngo5 zung1-ji3 tai2 syu1 do1-gwo3
        haang4-gaai1

(我鍾意睇書多過行街。)

Chapter 10

1.   go3 (個)

2.   zek3 (隻)

3.   deoi3 (對)

4.   ngo5 tau4 tung3 (我頭痛)

5.   jau5 siu2-siu2 tau4-tung3 (有少少頭痛)

        have a little headache

6.   ngo5 sap6 dim2 fan3 gaau3

        What time do you get up?

        I am brushing my teeth now.

        keoi5 zou6 gan2 me1 aa3

        I am having a stomachache (and) not going to work.

Chapter 11

1.   no

2.   gam1-jat6 ge3 tin1-hei3 dim2 aa3? (今日嘅天氣點呀?)

3.   ceon1 (春) - spring

   haa6 (夏) - summer

   cau1 (秋) - fall

   dung1 (冬) - winter

4.   daa2 (打)

5.   tek3 (踢)

6.   Draw a line to connect the appropriate Chinese character to its translation:

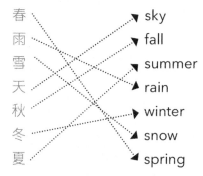

7.   Today's weather is very good.

   ngo5 zeoi3 zung1 ji3 haa6 tin1

   Hong Kong's winter doesn't (have) snow.

Chapter 12

1.   gwaan1 mun4 (關門)

2.   to save

3.   eco-friendly

4.   when, used in a statement

5.   I am very frugal.

        How can you save money?

        nei5 uk1-kei2 jau5-mou5 haan1 din6 daam2 aa3?

        ngo5 jau5 waan4 bou2 kap1 gun2

Part IV Review: Winter

1.   ngo5 tou5 tung3

2.   Your eyes are very big.

3.   In winter, I like to drink hot milk tea.

References

Cheung, Samuel Hung Nin 張洪年. A Grammar of Cantonese as Spoken in Hong Kong (revised ed.). Hong Kong: The Chinese University Press, 2007. Print.

"Hong Kong Lags Behind in Workplace Gender Equality, Says the Women's Foundation CEO." By Mallika Kapur. Bloomberg Markets: Asia. Bloomberg. New York, 5 Nov. 2019. Television.

Li, Emil 李嘉亮. 粵讀粵有趣. Hong Kong: New Talent Press, July 2015. Print.

Linguistic Society of Hong Kong. Jyutping Word List, 2016. Web. 22 Jul. 2017.

Liu, Lening 劉樂寧. "Chinese syntax and morphology." Teaching Chinese to Students of Other Languages. Beijing Language and Culture University. Jul. 2016. Lecture.

Tang, Sze-Wing 鄧思穎. Lecture on Cantonese Grammar. Hong Kong: The Commercial Press, Jul. 2015. Print.

Acknowledgements

I want to thank many people from the bottom of my heart because this book would not have become a reality without your continuous love, support, and contribution.

To **Man Wa Kwong**, for always being a supportive friend who is also extremely knowledgeable in Chinese education. Thank you for generously offering your expertise in teaching Cantonese and tips for living in Hong Kong. I am greatly humbled by you.

To **June Pham**, for the simple and structured layout design that makes the book fun and engaging for readers. Your never-ending encouragement and diligence motivate me to constantly grow and make progress on each book we work on together.

To **Carmen Yeung**, not only for editing this book, but also for being a great friend who always patiently listens and understands my words beyond their literal meaning.

To **Kimberly Newell**, for always supporting the work I do and the causes I care about. Your curiosity for learning and attention to detail never cease to amaze me.

To the **Writing Center at Baruch College**, for the resources provided to me while editing my early drafts.

To **Jasmine Xu**, for your beautiful illustrations that gave life to Book 1 and furthered the love of the language to many others. You made Book 2 possible.

To **Alison Cohen**, my lifelong teacher, friend, and inspiration, for your kindness and encouragement. Thank you for constantly reminding me of the joy I find in teaching, and following my heart to continue writing.

To **Xin Lin**, for always having faith in me and my work, even at times when I didn't believe in myself. Your support is the bedrock of our friendship.

To **Ruth Kevess-Cohen**, for your never-ending kindness and encouragement to me. I will always trust you to be my first reader and implement your useful advice to provide as many resources as I can to the readers.

To **my parents**, who will semantically understand the half of this book that is written in Chinese and are wise enough to guess the rest, for your all-surpassing support and sacrifice in this country, so that I could become a better me.

To **all of my students**, for always reminding me that learning a new language as an adult is not easy, and for always teaching me how to become a more sympathetic teacher.

To **my support group in faith**, for your unconditional fellowship in every aspect. You have witnessed my highest highs and lowest lows and strengthened me through every project I have done.

About the Author

Photo credit: Qihong Jiang

Jade Jia Ying Wu completed her Teaching Certificate Program in TESOL (Teaching English to Speakers of Other Languages) and TCSOL (Teaching Chinese to Speakers of Other Languages) from Teachers College, Columbia University and Beijing Language and Culture University in 2016. She has taught Chinese in classrooms of various sizes and to students of all ages, in both the U.S. and China. She holds a bachelor's degree in statistics and quantitative modeling from Baruch College, City University of New York.

Jade was born and raised in Guangdong, China, where Cantonese is one of the main dialects. She moved to Swartz Creek, Michigan at the age of thirteen and spent most of her young adulthood living in New York City. Experiencing both Chinese and American cultures, she was often confused yet fascinated by the differences between them. In 2014, she created her website InspirLang to teach Cantonese, Mandarin, and Taishanese to non-native speakers, and developed her own Romanized system for Taishanese. She currently hosts language podcasts such as: Learn Cantonese Daily, Cantonese Diaspora, Learn Mandarin Daily, and Learn Taishanese Daily. A former instructor at CUNY, she is also the author of *Learn to Speak Mandarin I: A Beginner's Guide to Mastering Conversational Mandarin Chinese.*

In her free time, Jade also enjoys learning other languages such as Spanish, French, and Korean. She lives in Brooklyn, New York.

www.inspirlang.com

www.inspirlang.com/rssfeed

@InspirLang

More from Jade

Learn to Speak Cantonese 1
Paperback and ebook available

Imagine falling in love with someone, but not speaking the same language as their extended family. This is the case for Gabriel, the narrator of this textbook, who is an American boy learning Cantonese to impress his girlfriend's mom. In this Cantonese learning book, you will join Gabriel in his first meeting with Jenny's mother, who is from Hong Kong and can only speak Cantonese. From having dim sum to describing his favorite pastimes, Gabriel will teach you everything you need to know to master basic conversational Cantonese.

Learn to Speak Mandarin 1
Paperback and ebook available

Imagine you have found your dream job at a company that is located in a different country, but you don't speak the language of that country. This is the case for An An, the narrator of this textbook. An An is a brave panda from Washington, D.C. who learned Mandarin and traveled across the world to Beijing for his dream job interview. In this book, you will join An An for 10 hours (chapters) for his first day in Beijing going to his job interview and learning to speak Chinese in a variety of settings.

An An will teach you everything you need to know to master basic conversational Mandarin. Follow along as he introduces himself to the job interviewer, describes his favorite pastimes, and as he meets his dream significant other, panda Ping Ping. Ranging from asking for directions, to communicating with the taxi driver in Mandarin while learning how to count, each lesson combines cultural insights about Chinese traditions and customs alongside basic language instruction.

Made in the USA
Las Vegas, NV
07 December 2023